THE SECRET SCIENCE OF GAMES

JOHN HOPSON

CONTENTS

PREFACE

This is a biased book about an objective profession. For two decades I've had the privilege of being a professional games researcher, collaborating with the best game developers in the world on some of the most successful games of all time. In an industry where everyone is passionate about their individual creative viewpoint, my role has been to act as a neutral conduit for the player voice, to set my personal opinions aside and advocate for the people who played our games.

However, while I try to stay objective when working on the games themselves, I find myself being very judgmental about how we talk to people about games research. We mostly try to be too formal, too pseudo-academic, and generally make things more complicated than they should be. Given how much time games researchers spend working on tutorials, you'd think we'd be better at them.

This book is intended as an entertaining and accessible introduction to the real role I've seen research play in the games industry. It contains my core principles, advice I give new researchers on my team, some good stories, and the practical lessons I've learned from my professional successes and failures over the past twenty years. It's what I've used make each of my games a little bit better.

I hope it helps.

John Hopson

PART ONE
FOUNDATIONS

CHAPTER 1
A RESEARCHER'S DEFINITION OF FUN

My job is to make games more fun. Not all games have to be fun, of course, but the ones I've worked on are popular entertainment. On blockbuster titles like *Halo, Age of Empires, Destiny, World of Warcraft,* and *Hearthstone,* my personal contribution has been to help the development team understand when players are having fun.

"Fun" is one of those dense little words like "love" that provoke a lot of debate about their precise definition. Everyone's got an opinion, and people talking about fun get into arguments using big, impressive concepts like *immersion, flow,* and *autonomy*. Smart people have written scholarly books on fun, subdivided it into categories, and tried to copyright their personal formulations.

Those debates can be interesting to read, but I've worked on a lot of great games and my definition of fun is extremely simple:

Fun is whatever the designer and player agree is fun.

I'm completely serious; this is not a cop-out or a joke. It's a practical and functional definition, one that enables me to skip all the debate and get right down to the important business of making better games.

The beauty of this approach is that it divides the world into a neat set of four categories:

	Things the designer intended to be fun	**Things the designer didn't intend to be fun**
Things the player says are fun	Expected fun	Unexpected fun
Things the player says are not fun	Unexpected non-fun	Expected non-fun

Every experience the player has in a game will fall into one of those four boxes. My role as a user researcher is to determine where each experience currently sits and see to it that any mismatches are corrected.

Now, the easiest category is, of course, the upper left, where the player is having fun in exactly the way the designer intended. This is wonderful, we can all go home early.

The bottom right category is nearly as straightforward. If the player says something they're doing isn't fun and the designer says it was never intended to be fun, then we're still in good shape. We probably need to discuss why this not fun thing is even possible in the game or why the player went there, but the world is fundamentally functioning the way it should and the designer's intuition is being upheld. It's the other two categories that require the most additional analysis. Let's take a closer look at each of them.

UNEXPECTED FUN

My favorite category is the upper right: the "Unexpected Fun" moments when our players discover ways to have fun that the game makers never imagined.

A good example of this kind of fun is Gandhi. (Not a commonly expressed sentiment, I admit.) In the *Civilization* series, nations compete through war, trade, and diplomacy, and part of the charm of the game is that each nation is led by a famous historical figure, such as George Washington for America, Queen Elizabeth I for England, and Mahatma Gandhi for India. In keeping with his nonviolent protests against British rule in India, the AI for Gandhi was set to be the most peaceful possible. However, under certain circumstances, Gandhi's aggression would drastically increase, transforming him from a pacifist into the game's most warlike ruler.

To the designers' surprise, this counter-factual version of the character turned out to be more fun than the original. Players loved the dissonance of being threatened with nuclear war by a historical pacifist. They weren't having the intended experience, but the experience they were having was awesome and the designers made the correct call to just roll with it. Even in current versions of the game, many years later, Gandhi still feels more likely to nuke you than any of the other opponents.

These are the best moments in making a game, when players find fun that the game's creators never intended and the designers choose to encourage it. Games user research can be a key part of this process, helping to identify all the ways that players are spending their time so that the designers can choose which ones to support.

UNEXPECTED NON-FUN

Unfortunately, much of my games research work focuses on the bottom left corner of the grid, where players are not receiving the intended experience and are not having fun. While I'm using the word "fun" here, this approach works for every aspect of game design. I could just as easily substitute "difficulty" for "fun," comparing how many times players died in a mission to how many times the designer predicted they would or look at how the weapons the player uses in a particular mission match up with what the mission's makers assumed they would ahead of time.

This definition of fun is a special case of the larger goal of user research: *verifying designer intent*. Game designers always have a vision in their minds of an experience that they want players to have, and they craft a complex software machine intended to engender that experience. That machine is inevitably flawed, and many of those flaws can only be revealed when a typical player experiences the game without outside help. This is because even the most skilled designer cannot erase all preconceptions, knowledge, and assumptions from their mind. The designer knows that the shotgun is supposed to be a close-range weapon in this game, so they never get frustrated that it does minimal damage at long distance. They know that doors require color-coded keys, so they won't waste hours trying to figure out how to open a door without one. Designers glide through their own games along the optimal path, but that path is not always obvious to the rest of us.

My primary job as a games industry researcher is to identify where and when the player experience will differ from the design intent. Of course, on a good day I also find out how and why it differs, but those are secondary goals. In my experience, very few user experience issues are mysteries. Designers are generally pretty good at diagnosing problems once an issue is brought to their attention, so my role as a researcher becomes detecting when a problem is occurring and gauging how badly it impacts the player experience.

THERE IS NO "I" IN "USER RESEARCH"

Finally, you'll note that my personal opinion of what's fun does not appear anywhere in this definition. That's because I don't get to have an opinion. There have been times in my career where I've had very strong thoughts on a certain character or mission but shaping the game to match those opinions is antithetical to my job. Designers are drowning in a sea of opinions. Everyone tells them that things are too hard, too easy, paladins need to be nerfed, and they should really add one more little feature…

To stand out and make an impact, a games user researcher must be different. I absolutely cannot be just one more interchangeable opinion. Research must bring something new to the table, a unique value proposition to justify my inclusion in an already complex development process.

My neutrality is not a burden; it's a superpower. It's what allows my designers to trust me, and that trust is what allows my research to have impact. Even the most insightful research study can founder on the rocks of "why should we believe you?" By constraining myself in this way, I enable a unique relationship with my designers. It's analogous to doctor-patient confidentiality, where a guarantee of privacy allows the patient to be more honest and therefore receive more accurate medical care. My neutrality creates trust, trust lets the designers engage with my research, the research brings the game closer to the intended experience, players have more fun. Designers must believe the research for the research to produce to a better user experience, and that can't happen if they're second guessing the researcher's motives.

Designers want to achieve their creative vision; players want to have fun. This book is about how games user researchers work behind the scenes to help make both those things happen.

CHAPTER 2
A SIMPLE FORMULA FOR BETTER GAMES

The Scarab is an alien vehicle used by the Covenant enemies in the *Halo* series, one of the first franchises I ever worked on. It's basically a hundred-foot-tall robot spider with a laser cannon for a mouth. One significant concern that came up during the design process for the Scarab was the actual mechanics of a tiny human protagonist fighting a giant spider robot.

Would players try to get on top? Would they roll underneath and attack from below like Luke Skywalker in *The Empire Strikes Back*? Would they snipe at the joints or the vehicle's crew from a distance? Would they assume it couldn't be killed at all and just avoid it? Making any or all of these options work would require a big investment of resources by the studio, so anything we could do to understand how players would react would help lessen the risk.

The approach we took was to run a series of individual play sessions very early on in development. There was no success or failure in this test; we were just seeing what happened. We actually ran this test so early that most of the game's graphics weren't even present. The ground was just a featureless gray plain, and the rocket launcher was nothing but an untextured set of blocks. But players could see the Scarab, it could move around and attack, and we could see how the player reacted. That was all that was necessary.

This test had no tasks and no way to win; we just put the player in the situation and watched. As it turned out, most players wanted to be able to attack from a distance, but our intended weak points on the Scarab's knees weren't apparent to our early testers. We added extra glowing bits to the joints in the final vehicle model and made it more obvious that damage to the knees was super effective.

I don't think I ever wrote a report for this study. The designer responsible for the Scarab sat with me in the lab for a couple of days, watched players battle his creation, and walked away with a head full of ideas for ways to make the fight more epic. The player played, the designer watched, the game got better.

My entire job as a games user researcher can be boiled down to that same simple formula:

Have a real player play the game and get the people who made the game to watch.

Everything else is gravy. The fundamental truth of a game is what happens when a real person plays the thing. The best use of that truth is to feed the decision-making process of the person who made the thing. That's the most important message I can write. You can close the book now; we're done here.

OK, maybe you shouldn't stop here. But that definition of my profession is completely true. The trouble is, it's one of those "easy to say, hard to execute" situations. Let's unpack the component parts and walk through them individually.

First, by "**real player**" I mean "someone who will have the same experience as the players who play the game after release." The people who make games are not normal and don't react to their own games the way the average player will. User research is about finding ways to bring the perspectives of normal players into the development process as early and often as possible. There can be lots of debates about who the target players for a game are, but any widening of perspective beyond the development team is beneficial.

By "**play the game**" I mean "provide an approximation of how players will respond to the game after release." A lot of my research occurs when a game is not actually fun or even playable in the normal sense. I can test concept art, paper prototypes of the user interface, and other components of a game before they're expensively built and assembled into a coherent experience. There can be tons of value gained from testing a game that isn't done yet, if the testing is handled correctly. The further away we are from a traditional playthrough, the more creative we have to be to collect good feedback and the more cautious we have to be in interpreting the results.

By "**get the people who made the game to watch**" I mean "use the player experience to affect the decision makers." Decisions in game development are almost never made by the person doing the research, and you really wouldn't want them to be. While the largest impact almost always comes from a direct real-time viewing, written reports, video clips, debrief meetings, and other proxies are all ways to communicate the user experience to the development team. And of course, the real test of any researcher is to push the team to act on what they see. There's no medal for running the most research; the only thing that counts is improving the game.

There's a wide variety of methods in games user research, some quite complicated, and I'll discuss many of them in this book. But all of them boil down to some variation of getting a real person to play the game and getting the people who made the game to pay attention. If those three components are present, the game will get better. There are certainly better and worse ways to run a research study, but any study that honestly represents the intersection of player, game, and creator has the potential to produce positive change in the game.

I'm not saying this to dumb down games research. As I described in the Scarab example above, I've run these sorts of simple observational studies myself on big budget games which have gone on to great success. It is very common to encounter situations in game development where the right answer, even for an experienced researcher with a complete toolbox of sophisticated methods and money to burn, is to just put a player in contact with the game and see what happens.

That's the fundamental alchemy of user research, and it's why I'm comfortable making this book accessible and not adhering to a particular research doctrine. Games research doesn't necessarily have to follow a rigid methodology to benefit the game. If the magical combination of player, game, and game maker are present, a prospective researcher will be on the right track.

CHAPTER 3
THE PERFECT PLAYER

The first thing every participant in my studies does is apologize for not being a real gamer. They assume that what I'm looking for are authoritative opinions from a connoisseur, insightful diagnoses of how to fix the game. This is a fundamental misunderstanding of the point of user research, even though I state it explicitly up front in every session:

"We're not testing you, we're testing the game."

Participants always feel like they're the ones being tested, when in reality *they are the test*. They're the wind tunnel, not the plane. It's not called "user research" because I'm doing research *on* users; I'm deploying users to do research on the game. The performance of the players in a study is only interesting for what it tells me about the game. Each player is a sonar pulse sweeping across the game's design and hopefully pinging back to me with interesting data. Those return pings are simultaneously failures for the participant and successes for the study—and for me as the researcher.

This is all to say that I actually need the players in my studies to fail. The best way to discover problems in the game is if those problems interfere with the player experience while I'm watching. Literally the worst outcome in a games user research study is when the player skates flawlessly through the entire test. It's very hard to draw conclusions from that. Were there really no problems, or did the player just happen to bypass them? If a gifted or lucky player beats a boss fight on the first try, it doesn't tell us whether it may still be too hard for most players.

At the same time, I don't want the player to fail too hard. If a participant is completely stumped by the basic controls, that means I won't have a chance to learn anything beyond that initial problem. There is an ideal level of participant failure. In a good study, players are slowed but not stopped, confused but not stumped. I want participants to experience just enough failure to clearly mark the problem and convince the dev team it needs to be fixed, but not so much that I have to intervene and disrupt the natural flow of play.

Similarly, I want players to experience different degrees of failure on different parts of the game. If a player can't figure out anything, it can be too easy for a designer to dismiss that player's feedback entirely. For the best feedback, the player needs to succeed at some things but not others. If I test a single mission and players die four times each, it can be hard to draw conclusions as to whether that was too hard or too easy. If I test multiple missions and players die twice as often in one as the others, now I've got some contrast to work with. The conversation with the development team shifts from "the game is too hard" to "why is that mission so much harder than the others?" The latter is much likelier to lead to a productive discussion and a better game.

Another consideration is the participants' emotional experience during the study. I don't want the study to be just a wall of continuous failure;

of problems that plague most games in development are exactly the kind that fall through the cracks when you're overly familiar with the game.

These problems are not the ones that designers dream about dealing with when they're training for their career. They're not about creative vision or a big new idea; they're not fun to debate or brainstorm ways to fix. They won't be discovered or solved in a brilliant moment of auteur insight. They're the gaming equivalent of sand in the gears, a flat tire, pimples, or the flu. In other words, they're just the inevitable yet everyday flaws of a human creation. This is good news, because it means that fixing them is much less controversial than directly challenging the core of the game's design. The car's design is still good, I'm just helping them find the tire that needs more air.

Before I start talking about the details of how research is done, it's important to have a sense of what kinds of problems I'm trying to detect and fix. Here's a sample set of real issues from a few of the games I've worked on, all of which were discovered and fixed during development.

HALO

- Players didn't realize they could pick up new weapons and found themselves at a disadvantage as they progressed through the game with just the starter weapon.

- Players didn't get in a vehicle at the right point in the mission, instead making a long, boring walk to the next fight.

DESTINY

- Players didn't spend their talent points, limiting their characters and making the rest of the game much harder.

- Players accidentally destroyed weapons when trying to equip them, leaving them with much worse gear than designers anticipated.

WORLD OF WARCRAFT

- Players didn't realize which enemies they were meant to attack and attacked something much higher level which killed them instantly.

- Players couldn't find the quest giver because he was on a different floor of the building, leaving them to wander back and forth and making them unable to progress the story.

These examples all have a few things in common:

- **These are all massively successful games made by amazing, highly experienced teams.** It doesn't matter how good the dev team is; games are such complex entities with so many moving parts that there are inevitably rough places for a researcher to find and fix.

- **The problems are boring.** It doesn't take a dramatic issue to cause players to quit; it just has to be enough to keep them from having the fun they came for.

- **None of these would be problems for the people who made**

the game. If you know the answer ahead of time, you wouldn't experience any of these issues.

- All these problems result in the player having less fun. They are not necessarily about in-game actions that are fun in themselves, but they interfered with players accessing the fun of the game.

- The root causes of the problems are all different. They represent a range of design failures. But they all manifest in a straightforward manner, blocking the ability of players to progress smoothly through the game.

There are people out there who claim to have formal structures for analyzing games, usually with a snappy acronym and an expensive consulting service. But in my experience shipping dozens of successful games, the problems are almost always relatively straightforward once detected. That's why my research methods could be described primarily as ways of detecting problems, with understanding the frequency / scope of a problem and diagnosing their causes being secondary objectives.

I'm not looking for subtle, sophisticated problems. I'm looking for big chunky things that are blocking the fun. That's why it's all right to use big chunky methods like "talking to people" (interviews) or "watch person play game" (usability). There are always tons of issues to be found and fixed in every game. The methods I'm discussing here are fairly straightforward because we're looking for fairly straightforward problems.

Beneath terminology and more complicated methods, games research is pretty simple at its core. If the problem is really there in the game, it will show up in any honest testing. The fine details of which method to use and how it's executed are less important than honestly listening to our players.

CHAPTER 5
CHAOS AND THE GRUNTS OF DEATH

During the development of *Halo 3*, I ran one particular playtest where the players just kept dying, over and over. I asked the designers what they'd changed, and they swore that nothing was different, and that I must have just gotten a bad batch of players this week. The fact remained that the participants were dropping like flies, way too often to be due to chance. So, I investigated.

Most of the additional deaths were in one section of one mission, a large outdoor area with lots of vehicles. When I drilled in and looked at the video recordings for the deaths, most of them were due to Grunts, the weakest enemy in the game. Every video ended with the player's body lying on the ground, with Grunts in vehicles zooming back and forth over their corpse. (In *Halo 3*'s campaign, enemies don't stop attacking once the player dies, but instead will keep shooting at their body or, in this case, keep trying to ram it with their vehicles.)

As it turned out, our designers were right: They hadn't changed a single thing about the mission design. There was a bug that caused any

Grunt who got into a vehicle to switch to the maximum difficulty "Legendary" AI. Even if the player was playing on the easiest setting, when a Grunt got into a vehicle, they turned into killing machines. They instantly developed perfect accuracy and maximum aggression and would hunt the player with Terminator-like focus. We called them "the Grunts of Death."

One reason this bug survived long enough to make it into the playtest was that it was a lot less apparent during internal playtests or QA tests. Our skilled professionals generally didn't allow the Grunts to survive long or let them get into abandoned vehicles. The bug created an unintentional difficulty spike that only really punished inexperienced players.

It's also important to realize that this scenario was nothing that could have been anticipated beforehand. It wasn't part of the written design of the level or the architecture of the code. Even the Grunts' AI worked as expected, except in the unique case where a player with below average skill played on a lower difficulty setting and allowed these particular enemies to get in a vehicle.

It was an emergent phenomenon, something that only happened when all the pieces (including normal, non-professional players) came together. In this case, the problem was due to a bug. But there are countless other times when equally bad experiences are created even when everything is technically working perfectly.

Truth is what happens when a real player plays the game. Every other part of the creation process is fantasy: Every brilliant design document, every beautiful creative idea from a developer, every insightful marketing pitch, even the lines of code and data files that make up the game... none of them are true. The only true things are what real players do and feel when they play the game. My job as a researcher is to inject that reality into the design process, to cut through all the ambitious dreams and fantasies of development with the harsh truth of actual player experience. Obviously, this makes me very popular with my colleagues.

Games are a multi-billion-dollar industry with revenues rivaling those of acknowledged cultural giants like movies and television. It is completely reasonable for an industry of that size to want predictability. If you're going to spend hundreds of millions of dollars developing and marketing a game, it'd be nice to know how it all will turn out ahead of time.

Unfortunately, games and their players are inherently unpredictable. This is not unique to games, but we tend to buy into the myth of designer as all-controlling mastermind, believing that a good design can perfectly channel the player into an ideal pattern of behavior. But any designer (particularly when they've had a few drinks) will tell you that players do weird things. Players are infinitely creative, finding ways to improve or ruin their own experiences no matter how tightly the game tries to constrain them.

At the same time, the games themselves are incredibly complex pieces of software, often made by teams of hundreds or thousands of people and consisting of millions of lines of code. When that complexity is mixed with large numbers of players interacting with the game and each other, the result is inherently unpredictable.

In chaos theory, there is the concept of sensitivity to initial conditions, also known as the "butterfly effect." It means two situations can look nearly identical, but that small changes in the starting circumstances can result in dramatically different outcomes. Those small differences can have larger and larger effects over time, which is why weather forecasting is fairly accurate for this afternoon but can be wildly off for next month. This can be true even if every individual step in the process is deterministic and predictable. Small predictable differences can add up over time into something radically different than expected.

A lot of user experience work aims to understand and implement design patterns. Our logic is that we shouldn't be reinventing game design from scratch every time, because human behavior follows understandable rules. If we pay attention, we should be able to take a design and forecast what the player experience will be based purely on studying the successes and failures of past designs.

That idea is not totally wrong: people's reactions are broadly predictable and that's a good thing. Imagine how terrible it would be if every person's response to food was completely different from the person next to them or compared to their own tastes of the day before. Without at least a little consistency, design wouldn't ever be able to move past that initial discovery phase into more complex and interesting ideas. And it's certainly true that we should start development with a game design informed by successful historical patterns.

But the devil is in the details and (as in the *Halo* story above) many of those details don't manifest until the game is played by its intended audience. It's possible to make a horrible game out of good parts. The way a design principle is implemented can radically change its impact on the player experience.

No matter how good our design patterns or how well we learn from other titles, there will always be a step for "put the game in front of real people and see what happens." That's what user researchers do.

It's also true that even when the principles are both tested and well-understood, they're hard to enforce. Anyone who's ever tried sticking to a diet knows that. Just as I can talk myself into eating an extra doughnut, game developers can easily fool themselves into deviating from their own intended best practices.

For example, everyone knows that sudden increases in difficulty are bad; every designer in the world will claim to avoid them. But things happen. A weapon's stats can be tweaked in a way that doesn't matter 99% of the time, but in this one fight makes a huge difference. A key early encounter is removed, a skill isn't taught, and the player has a very different game experience. Even where the goals are understood and followed in good faith, small changes can radically alter outcomes.

I'm not here to tell my designers how to make a good game. They already know how to do that. I'm here to hold them to their own goals. Good user research shows them where they've failed to live up to their own standards, just as a therapist or coach might offer constructive observations. My designers are not wrong; they're imperfect people working in an incredibly complex medium. Frankly, we should be amazed that any game plays anything like its original intent.

This unpredictability is why I find games fascinating, both as an entertainment medium and a profession. It's why games user research is a vital part of the development process, and why my job as a researcher is both simple and endless. The combination of complex software, human creativity, and the uniqueness of each game's implementation mean that there is always something to find. We could test the same game a hundred times, fixing every problem every time, and still not reach perfection.

Hire the most brilliant designers in the world, and there will still be issues to find in the lab. Spend months in preproduction, making sure the plan is perfect, and there will still be user experience problems that make players cry in frustration. But there will also be moments where players experience new fun, where the pieces come together to create moments of joy that no one could have made on purpose. It is not possible to design a perfect game—and that is a wonderful thing.

CHAPTER 6
SHAPING BEHAVIOR

For my entire career in games, I've been contacted every few months by some reporter or other wanting to do a story about how I use my eldritch psychology powers to make games addictive. They're suffering from the misconception that the games industry employs psychologists to warp the way players think to companies' advantage. The truth is exactly the opposite: **I'm here to shape the way the company thinks to suit the needs of the players.**

Companies make terrible decisions when isolated from their customers. Worse, they often don't realize that those decisions are out of touch with reality until way too late. In the day-to-day chaos of game development, it's easy to make decisions that reflect more immediate pressures rather than making a game that works for its eventual players.

This is not because of anything nefarious. Everyone has biases, everyone has deadlines, and some things are harder to do than others. It's natural that the development process might gravitate toward solving the needs of the development team rather than the needs of the end user. One of those development needs is shipping the best possible game, but it's far from the only one. Sure, there are players out there somewhere in the future who will eventually be impacted by what we're making but keeping your boss happy and hitting the milestone dates can seem a lot more important in the moment. Everyone always wants to make a good game, but the definition of "good" at any given moment is subject to a lot of implicit biases. When you're buried in the everyday details of bringing a game to life, it's hard to maintain an clear perspective about the final product.

Games user research is an essential part of the solution to this problem. My role as a user researcher is to inject the player voice into the design conversation as early and as often as possible. In a perfect world, every decision would be made with a clear-eyed understanding of how that decision will impact the final player experience.

This can be tricky because a lot of decisions are necessarily made before the game is in a state where it can be put in front of normal users. But while they can't play the game before it actually exists, I can make sure that the decision makers have the best information available. I can test competitors, prototypes, or individual features from other games that give insight into the thing the studio is thinking of building.

These proxies for our game may not always be exact or straightforward, but they're a thousand times better than just guessing. My methods don't have to be perfect. They just have to be better than the development team's natural state of well-intentioned isolation. That's not a high bar.

Compromise is a necessary factor in development. Games always start with a vision that's glorious, expansive, and completely unshippable. It's much easier to imagine cool stuff than to actually build it. It is a fundamental fact of the industry that every development team discovers that they need to modify their plan along the way. This isn't something that can be avoided through research; it's necessary for the game to survive until release. The point of including the player perspective in the discussion is to ensure that the inevitable compromise is made with full information. The player voice, in the form of user research, must be in the room.

"But wait," my designers cry, "we already know what players like! That's why we're the designers!" To which I say, "kinda." Designers do have a pretty accurate picture of player priorities in their heads, but what makes them special is all the other stuff in their heads. Being a successful designer takes a lot of other skills and knowledge beyond just knowing fun when they play it. As vital as those extra things are, they can also interfere with decision making.

For example, designers know the limitations of their tools, and will naturally gravitate towards solutions that work within those tools. Repositioning a character is easy and changing the character's appearance is hard, so they'll suggest the former over the latter. They're not necessarily wrong to make that decision, but the ease of that solution may subconsciously skew their judgment.

This is one reason I believe it's valuable to have people like me who are full-time researchers rather than hybrid UX researcher/designers. I never have to execute my solutions. Like a defense attorney, I am free to advocate passionately and unreservedly for the player perspective. Someone has to. And someone else must be the judge and decide what action will ultimately be taken. The player perspective, as advocated for by the research team, shouldn't always win, but it should always be heard.

My focus on changing the company rather than the players is not just a matter of altruism. Players are squishy and complicated and there's a billion pressures on them that I can't control. There's this conspiratorial notion that designers and psychologists are manipulative masterminds, perfectly channeling the players into desired patterns of behavior, but nothing could be farther from the truth.

Players can and do break the design of every single game they play. I've shipped games where we were totally clear in our intent, provided obvious signposts, and laid out every possible reward for playing "correctly," only to watch players find a way to do their own thing. If it were easy to shape human nature for millions of people, the world would be a much better-organized and creepier place.

In contrast, game companies are finite. There's a comparatively small number of decision-makers working on my games, and I can personally meet with and persuade each of them. I can customize my arguments to these specific individuals, choosing exactly the words and methods that will convince them. It's an achievable goal. Game companies are also more or less rational. My company will change its behavior if I can express player needs in terms the company understands.

What's even better is that institutional-level solutions have some staying power. If I can build research and the user perspective into my company's process, I win not only the current battle but make it easier to win all the similar fights in the future.

Shaping the company to better serve our players is the goal researchers can and should strive for. Unlike shaping players, it's a battle we can actually win and which can stay won.

Nothing in this book will tell you how to make players do anything they don't want to do. We can't control our players. We can only control what's in the game. My job is to show what happens when the thing we can control (game design) mixes with the thing we can't control (human nature), and then *change the design*. The original plan for the game is a fantasy, but what players do and say when in contact with what we built is real. The game must adapt to them, not the other way around.

I am not here to fix players because they are not broken. If players don't use the intended weapon, they're correct. If they turn left where I thought they'd turn right, they're correct. The answers players give me are always true; my games just sometimes ask the wrong question.

My most basic function as a games researcher is to understand the match and mismatch between the design and the players, and then reshape the design. One step above that, I'm here to reshape the thinking of the people who create the design, to avoid the problems in the first place. And at a meta-level, I try to shape the thinking of the company (and the industry), to build a system that naturally takes the player perspective into account.

CHAPTER 7
SCIENCE-ISH

I call what I do *research,* my unit of work is a *study,* and I do my business in a *lab*. But this terminology conceals a terrible secret: a lot of what I do is not actually science. That's not a slam on either games research or science. I don't have to be doing science to make better games. Most of the people in the studio aren't doing science. They're still contributing to the game, and so am I.

"But Dr. Hopson," you might say, "you have that shiny PhD after your name!" That's true and it is very shiny, but what I do on a day-to-day basis isn't the experimental psychology I trained in. Instead, I use all the tools of psychology to run an applied process, more like what happens in a therapist's office than to what happens in a laboratory. The process of therapy uses background knowledge taken from psychological science, but the therapist isn't experimenting on their patients.

Another metaphor for what I do would be personal training. A personal trainer isn't doing science on their clients in the gym, they're adapting science-derived best practices to a particular client and holding the client accountable. Anyone who's done therapy, a workout plan, or even a diet will tell you that the hard part of self-improvement is not the science, it's the execution. The role of a user researcher (or a therapist, or a trainer, or a dietitian) is to guide their client through the process, helping them achieve their goals using tools provided by science.

However, the "help" is more important than the "science." Every client and game is different, and the job of a researcher is really to produce the most rigorous studies practical within the constraints of real world game development. A working games researcher's job is to help their team make better games. That process is informed by science, but it doesn't look much like what a pure scientist does. I believe that is a good thing

This all means that while I'm an experimental psychologist by training, only a very small fraction of my work in games has involved experiments. Most of my work is observational, because performing real experiments in gaming would often involve impractical logistics, like building two parallel versions of the game with different art styles. But when the stars align to create the right opportunity, games research lab experiments can be incredibly impactful.

Here's an example of a pure experiment that happened on FASA's *Shadowrun* game for the original Xbox. The *Shadowrun* universe is one of my favorites, and I was lucky enough to have a chance to help out a little towards the end of the game's development. In its Xbox incarnation, *Shadowrun* was a multiplayer shooter game, with players fighting each other with guns, technogadgets, and magic abilities.

Because the unique selling point of Shadowrun's gameplay was the combination of shooting and abilities, the guns couldn't be too effective. After all, if the best way to win a fight was with guns, players would never use the other cool abilities like summoning monsters, casting fireballs, and so on, and the game would end up feeling like every other shooter out there. However, this made the guns feel weak, since you were shooting someone and they weren't dying. A substantial portion of the team was pushing to increase the damage, with others pushing back in favor of the current weapon balance. The dissenting argument was that the actual time to kill was fine, but that there was insufficient feedback to players that they were doing damage. The arguments had become quite heated, and it was holding up development at a critical time.

In the end, Kris Moreno, the primary user researcher on the game, settled things with a proper science experiment. She had multiple randomized groups of players play matches under four different conditions:

- To establish a baseline, some groups played under a **default** condition, with no changes made to the core game.

- Some players experienced an **accuracy** condition, where we took out a lot of the randomness in the weapons and made them hit the target a lot more often.

- Some players experienced a **shield** condition, where they saw a translucent golden bubble appear around enemies when they were hit. This was intended to show that the bullets had hit the target, but that the target was at least partially protected and therefore the assailant wouldn't expect the target to fall dead instantly.

- Finally, there was the euphemistically named **enhanced feed-**

> **back** condition. This was an "M for mature"-rated game, so there was already going to be blood spray when someone was shot. But to make sure players got the point, the feedback condition in this study added a lot more blood—buckets of it. Honestly, I think the artists were kind of offended to be asked to create this condition, so they added a sarcastic amount of blood. Shooting someone would literally paint the wall behind them red, there was so much blood. We also increased the volume of the sounds each character made when they were shot, the amount of vibration in the controller, and the brightness of the muzzle flash.

Surprisingly, the core condition and the improved accuracy condition had nearly identical results. Actually making the guns better had no significant effect on player perception. Instead, players gave the weapons higher ratings in both the shield and feedback conditions. In fact, the highest ratings came when we tried a "combined" condition that had both shields *and* enhanced feedback. That resolved the problem to everyone's satisfaction, keeping the level of damage the same and improving the subjective impact of the guns.

This was an unusual circumstance, something that only made sense in the context of an otherwise unsolvable impasse on the development team. It is relatively rare for a research question in AAA game development to be tricky enough to justify building multiple gameplay conditions as happened in *Shadowrun*.

Despite the occasional experiment like the one I just described, most real scientists would cringe to call a games industry researcher's daily activities "science." Our work is sloppy and incomplete by the standards of academia, primarily due to the speed at which we operate. It's very normal for an academic research project to take months or years, while a game study that takes a few weeks is considered a major effort.

Real science is about proving that exactly one thing is going on, through systematic observation and experimentation. It's about placing a result in the context of a larger set of findings, building on a comprehensive model of the world. Games researchers, on the other hand, are generally trying to help their teams make immediate decisions. Building a model of the world is nice, but what we really need to know is "should we make this boss harder or easier?" or "can people figure out how to trade items with their friends?"

If what my games need is hard science, I'll do science. But most of what they really need is structured, accurate observations and feedback. Borrowing methods from real science provides that structure and accuracy, but that doesn't mean that user research is itself a science.

In fact, as someone who was once an academic scientist and is now a games researcher, I strongly believe that attempting to turn game development into a rigorous science would kill the medium. It would leave us with nothing but joyless, optimized game-shaped objects. The kind of designers or game studios that would let their design be driven purely by data would make bad games. No one works in the games industry by accident. We're here because we want to make something special, something glorious and new.

That's part of why I hate the phrase "data-driven," and prefer something more like "data-informed." The data cannot and should not make decisions for us, but it can help feed the fantastic process that goes on between the designers' ears. We don't need to automate the designers' job; we need to give designers better tools for understanding and shaping their own work. A sculptor isn't any less an artist if they use a better chisel, or even if they x-ray a block of marble before carving.

This chain of obligations derives from the route studies take to benefit the game:

-We run clean, ethical studies.

- Because the studies are managed correctly, they accurately reflect the final player experience.

- Understanding the player experience helps the team make better decisions.

- Making better decisions helps the company ship better and more successful games.

There is never a case where we want to short circuit that process by trying to improve game success (or to put it more bluntly, studio finances) without first helping design decisions. Similarly, any attempt to affect design decisions that isn't grounded in what players really think is doomed. That's why we must serve each of these masters in this order, starting from the most basic and working our way up to the larger considerations.

Here's how each step in the chain works:

THE PARTICIPANTS

My first and foremost obligation is to the participants in my lab. I have an absolute, written-in-blood duty to ensure that my participants are comfortable, happy, safe, and fairly compensated for their time.

Now, given that the job requires player failure to progress, I'm not guaranteeing players are always successful or that I'll answer all their questions. But I need to treat them like people, with genuine care and attention, before I can do anything else.

Beyond the ethical considerations, the reason this is at the foundation of the pyramid is that I cannot serve any of our other masters if I don't run safe, clean studies. If the participants aren't fundamentally OK with their lab experience, the data wouldn't be representative of the final game experience and there wasn't any point in running the study in the first place.

Respecting the participants is therefore the fundamental building block of the profession. If I don't serve my participants, I can't help anyone else. A study that doesn't treat its participants right will always produce bad data, leading to poor decisions and potentially a failed game.

THE PLAYERS

Second, I'm here to represent the interests of everyone who will play the game after release. That's the larger purpose of user research, injecting the post-ship player perspective into the pre-ship production process.

Of course, I want to help our development partners and the company. But I do that by surfacing the opinions of the players, and anything that obscures those opinions or shades them to suit the emotional needs of the dev team or the political needs of management is self-defeating.

My results must be true to the post-release player experience or they will drive bad decisions. Misrepresenting the player experience will always lead to heartbreak in the end, even if it makes the development team happy now. A researcher serves the team and the company best by being an honest advocate for the player.

THE TEAM

I'm here to help my development team make good decisions, take smart risks, and ship good games. This duty can quite often take the form of "tough love." What the team needs me to do is not always what they asked for, and what they need to hear from me isn't always pleasant. Even bad news serves the team, helping them make better decisions and better games.

The key here is that the measure of a study isn't the data, it's beneficial changes in the game. And the team will only make those changes if they trust that researcher is working in their best interest and honestly reporting the needs of the players in the study.

The history of user research in the games industry is littered with failed research teams. Lots of companies saw what was done at early pioneers like Microsoft and attempted to start their own programs, and many of those attempts fizzled out. Almost universally, the research teams that failed out early were the ones that served the company's leaders before the product team.

Don't get me wrong. Upper management support is essential to the long-term flourishing of a research team. But when research aligns itself with upper management at the cost of designer trust, we doom ourselves to irrelevance. If the actual developers on the front lines don't trust me, they won't act on my data. Without impact, the research team will wither away no matter how much executive support we have.

In extreme cases, I've run studies where I kept no records and written no report. The team was highly paranoid about the results of the study being used against them by management, so I made sure that was impossible by deleting every piece of data and every video recording as soon as the study was complete. The findings existed only in my mind and the members of the development team who came to watch.

By serving the team first, I made both the team and management happy. Sure, management would have been even happier in the short term if they'd received the grades as well as the impact, but the loss of trust from the team would have been more costly to management in the long term. The team wouldn't have been as willing to participate in the study or implement our findings, we would have shipped a worse game, and that would have been reflected in the larger game-level metrics that management cared about.

If the team is aligned with the company values, serving the team serves the company.

THE COMPANY

At the largest scale, game development is a business, and everyone at a game company is there to serve business goals. This includes research, even though our impact can be so diffuse as to be difficult to spot.

Aligning research to the higher-level needs of the company is often a question of choosing which research to do, rather than how to do the research. It's about knowing what matters to the business and using research to support those areas of the product.

However, once I choose an area to focus on, I go back to working bottom-up. The best way to serve the business on that topic is to help the team working on that topic, the best way to serve the team is to surface the player opinion on that topic, and the best way to collect accurate player opinions is to treat my lab subjects with respect.

CONFLICTING GOALS

Sometimes, there are situations in which research's duties to one constituency can come into conflict with another. For example, proving that a particular mission isn't fun for the general player population requires players in the lab to experience that mission and its lack of fun firsthand. Or sometimes the player base may have opinions that inevitably point the way towards changes that will make the design team unhappy.

When those conflicts occur, the higher-tier goals must give way. The best way to serve the company is to serve the product team, the best way to serve the product team is to honestly represent the needs of the players, and the best way to discover those needs is through good research studies that treat the participants like people.

There is no point in cutting corners here. Research can move mountains, but it does so by first and foremost respecting the players under our care. Happy player communities, empowered partners, and successful games are built on a foundation of honest, respectful research studies.

PART TWO
DOING RESEARCH

CHAPTER 9
WHY I HATE FUN

I mentioned earlier that it's my job to make sure games are fun. Accordingly, user researchers in the games industry are often asked to produce "fun scores" for games in development. These are overall grades for how well a game is doing and an indicator of review scores to come. Some publishers keep extensive databases of the fun ratings for every game they've tested, so they can say things like "this game is more fun than 95% of games." It's considered a key metric that can be plotted in a hopefully upward curve towards release, showing the improvement and quality of the game.[1]

As a professional games user researcher for over twenty years, I've asked some variation of "is this fun" many times and my games have generally scored well. In spite of that, I've come to consider overall fun ratings to be detrimental to the process of shipping a good game. Don't get me wrong: Fun is absolutely the most important attribute of my games. It's why I make games and it's why people play them. But I don't believe measuring the fun of a game as a whole is especially valuable in most circumstances.

My objection is not that fun is difficult to measure or that we shouldn't measure it. Simply asking players how much fun they're having is a reasonable first approximation of their experience, the same way asking someone if they're too cold or too hot is a good approximation of temperature. And scores for individual users can be useful in understanding what's working or not working in a game. But where we as an industry get into trouble is averaging player scores together into a single number to represent the game as a whole.

Here's why I hate average fun scores:

IT STOPS THE CONVERSATION

Once you give a game an overall score, the conversation ends. If it's a high score, the team pats themselves on the back and tunes out all the other issues, because how bad could they be? If it's a low score, they immediately start looking for reasons to dismiss the entire study: these weren't the target audience, they didn't play long enough to get to the fun part, etc. The bad score can't be true, so the entire test must be bad.

When you give an overall score to someone's game, you're judging everything they did on the game simultaneously; you're attacking (or buffing) their self-image as a developer. With smaller, more granular scores, it's easier for a creator to separate themselves from the project.

Overall fun scores block the conversation that's supposed to be the real purpose of testing a game in development. We don't just want to grade the game; we want to have an engaged, productive conversation about how it can be made better. Fun scores can inhibit that discussion.

IT'S NOT ACTIONABLE

When players say a game isn't fun, there's not a clear next step based on that statement alone. Sure, we want the game to be fun; that's what it's for. But just knowing it's not fun doesn't dictate a particular course of action. Does that mean it's too hard or too easy? Are players confused or bored? There's no "add more fun" button on my keyboard. The correct response to knowing a game isn't fun is to dig down into other data, looking for clues as to what the problem is. Since you're going to be doing that anyway, the fun question becomes redundant.

IT'S PARTICULARLY SUBJECT TO BIAS

People generally tell you to your face that the game is fun unless it's absolutely awful. Because fun is perceived to be the most important thing about a game, players who want to please their hosts will, at a bare minimum, say the game is fun.

This is especially true of the kind of in-house playtesting I do, where the participants know they're talking to the people who made the game. They've just walked up to a building with the studio's name on it and entered a lobby that's usually covered in gigantic prints of art from the game and a prominent case full of awards. It's unrealistic to expect a neutral position after that kind of buildup.

A bit of bias certainly isn't disqualifying in a playtester. People who are inclined to like a game will still have trouble figuring out the controls or navigating the game world. But an overall fun rating is exactly the sort of vague, holistic question that will be most affected by bias.

MULTIPLAYER FUN DOESN'T COUNT

Even Tic Tac Toe is fun if it's played with other people. The most boring activities in the world can be fun if there's another human involved. The fun generated by other people is something that would be equally true of any other game that group of friends could be playing. If your game is only fun when played with fun people, then it's not actually fun.

This is a particular challenge for games where the multiplayer mode is built first. Because AI tends to be a later addition to games, most games that intend to include both single player and multiplayer content tend to build the multiplayer first—and can easily fool themselves into thinking the game is fun when they really just enjoy playing with their coworkers. You can somewhat offset this effect by making sure the developers can't talk to each other during internal playtest, but there's still an inherent lift from playing with good people you know.

Now, I recognize that I'm an outlier on this topic. People in the games industry honestly want their games to be fun and expect their researchers to ask about it and provide an averaged metric. Here are a few suggestions for ways to better handle overall fun scores:

ASK IT, THEN SET IT ASIDE

There can be a lot of pressure to ask about fun. The players expect it, the team expects it, and if we don't ask it one of them will bring it up in a way that might sabotage the other goals of the study.

Therefore, sometimes the smartest thing we can do is ask up front for an overall evaluation of the game and then ignore it. Even if we do nothing with that data, asking it clears those general impressions out of the way and the participants' subsequent feedback will be much cleaner. They may even feel more comfortable about bringing up problems now that they've given a good overall grade.

Just because we asked it doesn't mean we have to emphasize the data from the question. Ask it early, then set it aside and dive into the details where the real work of making a better game happens. Don't make it the centerpiece of the study.

ASK IT LATER

There are many points in development where games simply aren't fun to play. And there are many parts of a game, such as menus, that aren't intended to be fun on their own. There are a lot of studies where fun isn't at issue, and we can simply put off asking about it until later in the development process. Saying "we're not testing for fun yet, that's something we'll do in a few months" has the advantage of being true (we do need to ask the question eventually) and less confrontational than straight up telling someone that asking about fun isn't helpful. The person making the request of you is correct; the timing just isn't right yet.

USE IT TO HELP THE TEAM ACCEPT THE REAL ISSUES

User research on a game can sometimes feel relentlessly negative, continually pointing out problems. To offset this, presentation of results should open with something positive and establish that we're all buddies on the same team before digging down into everything that needs to be fixed.

Sure, the overall fun score will be higher than it probably deserves to be. That's fine; just because it's not an accurate metric doesn't mean it can't be deployed to good effect. Put that nice high fun score up front to get everyone in a good mood, then go into all the details of what needs more work.

It's much easier for a development team to operate from a mindset of "it's fun but we still need to fix these things" rather than a mindset of "everything is awful." An inflated fun score can still serve the game by putting everyone in the right mental space for absorbing the harsher details.

ENABLE THE "BUT"

Participants often say "it's fun but…" as in "it's fun but a little confusing" or "it's fun but it's not for me." The second half of those statements can be extremely useful in making a better game even if the first part isn't. With that in mind, make it easy for people to qualify their overall statement by asking them the big fun question first, then ask all the little detail questions. Having given a good overall score, participants may be much more willing to criticize specific aspects of the game.

NARROW THE FOCUS

Similarly to the "fun but…" concept, asking about a narrow section of the game can make it easier for players to say critical things without feeling like they're criticizing the game makers. Players are willing to say "the game was fun, but this mission wasn't fun" or even "this mission was fun, but that one fight at the end wasn't fun." We just have to give them the chance to rate both the whole and the parts.

SCORE THE PLAYER, NOT THE GAME

One way to make fun scores valuable is not to analyze the overall average score, but to look at what differs between the players who said the game was very fun and those who said it was merely kinda fun. Did the ones who had fun use particular weapons? Did they have more prior experience in the genre? Travel around a different side of the map? Each of those differences is a clue into what parts of the game are working and what needs improvement. Mushing all the ratings together into an overall score misses the point. Different players have different experiences, and those differences hold the key to making a better game.

DETAILS MATTER

While we've been talking about fun, this argument applies to every type of global rating for a game. It doesn't matter if the game is fun as a whole, well balanced on average, or easy to learn in general. People keep playing or quit based on the experience they're having in the moment. We have to earn every second of ongoing player time as we go. A game can be good overall while still having giant potholes in the player journey. "It gets better later" is cold comfort to a player who isn't having fun now.

Games user research is at its best when it focuses on helping designers achieve their vision for the game. Directly grading that vision is counter to the spirit of the profession. Instead, we're most successful when we take the ultimate value of that vision as a given and frame our work in terms of discovering all the tiny places where players aren't experiencing the designers' intent. There's no prize for correctly grading the game, but making the game better has tangible rewards for the development team and the player.

It can seem paradoxical, but the best way to make a game fun overall is to ignore the overall fun of the game while it's in development. By setting aside the larger goal and perfecting the individual moments and mechanics, we produce something more than the fun of its parts.

CHAPTER 10
JUST ASK THEM

WHY I SHOULDN'T LISTEN TO PLAYERS

Games user research has borrowed a lot of tools (and people) from experimental psychology. Not needing to invent everything from scratch has given our field a tremendous head start, but it also brings along some historical baggage. It seemed obvious to early psychologists that the best way to study what someone was thinking was to just ask them. Early psychologists would conduct "experiments" where they exposed themselves to a stimulus (for example, being tickled) and then tried to observe and articulate their own thoughts in response. ("That felt more like an itch than a tickle to me.") Unfortunately, this sort of introspection is incredibly subjective and unreliable, and there was no good way to resolve conflicts where two psychologists disagreed about their internal experience.

In fact, introspection proved so unreliable that a subsequent major school of psychology, behaviorism, rejected the idea of internal mental states completely. "Screw this," they (metaphorically) said. "We're sticking to analyzing things which can be objectively observed." More recently, cognitive psychologists have spent decades measuring all the ways that our stated perceptions can be wrong.

Here are just a few of the many known issues with using self-report as a research tool:

Social Desirability. Players tend to give answers that make them look good. They're often unwilling to admit that a mission was too hard for them, for example, or that they resorted to online help to solve an in-game puzzle.

Affective forecasting. People in general are not very good at predicting how they will react emotionally to hypothetical situations. This makes it hard to get feedback on novel game designs before they're implemented. For example, players absolutely hated the matchmaking system for *Halo 2* when they were asked about it as a hypothetical situation. The idea that they couldn't control the map they were playing on or the precise game mode seemed just crazy to them. But once people experienced the system and the closely balanced and carefully curated games it provided, it became a huge success.

Memory. Generally, we ask players questions after they experience the game, which means they're relying on their memory to answer the questions. There are lots of issues with memory that can skew the answers we get. For example, when asked what they liked best about a mission, players are a lot more likely to remember moments from the beginning or end of a mission than moments in the middle.

I have a lot of personal sympathy for these arguments. When it comes down to it, I'm an introverted geek. I'm much more comfortable reviewing a player's data than asking them a question. However, I ask players what they think all the time and I've come to value it as a useful and effective tool.

WHY I LISTEN TO MY PLAYERS ANYWAY

Asking players directly what they think about a game is called "self-report" in research jargon, and it might surprise most people to learn that it is both the most common and the most controversial technique in games user research. If you ask a researcher what techniques they use, they'll go on and on about high-tech shiny stuff like analytics and eyetracking, with maybe an embarrassed mutter about questionnaires at the end. Almost anyone who does research on games uses self-report regularly, but we also regard it with a level of suspicion normally reserved for strange vans offering candy. I'm as guilty of this ambivalence as anyone else in the profession, but I'd like to take a little time to lay out why we have such a complicated relationship with self-report and why I believe it's still our single best research tool.

First, self-report is cheap, fast, and robust. It costs nothing, can be done under virtually any circumstances, and never breaks down. It works in the lab, on a home visit, or in a mass survey. It requires no setup, no technology, and can be analyzed quickly. As a *first approximation* of what a player is thinking, self-report goes a long way on very little effort.

In fact, self-report is so brutally, elegantly simple that it makes it hard for other methodologies to compete. I could attach electrodes to my participants' skin to measure their heart rate to see whether they're excited… or I could just ask them. I could buy an expensive eyetracker and bounce infrared beams off the participants' eyeballs to tell what they're looking at on the screen… or I could just ask them.

Now, I use a lot of those other methods too, because they really are more accurate than self-report and because I'm as fond of zapping my participants' eyeballs with infrared beams as the next nerd. But when I use them, it's because the specific research question requires that extra information and I almost always use them in conjunction with self-report.

Secondly, self-report is an incredibly *flexible* research tool. Almost any topic can be studied using some form of self-report. Weapon balance, level design, art style, AI behavior, I can ask players questions about nearly anything and get an answer. It may be an imperfect answer, but I can generally get something useful. In contrast, most other research tools are more specialized. Eyetracking might show that players are spending a lot of time looking at a particular character, but it won't tell us if that's because players admire the character or just hate his haircut. Datamining can't tell us anything about what players think of the artistic style of a game. Self-report isn't quite a universal method, but it's close.

Thirdly, the judgments we're asking for are within the understood margin of error for self-report. We're not looking for fine details of players' internal mental processes, but rather for general statements of emotional reaction. When a gamer says that a character was fun to play, that's a credible statement. Would I be willing to swear that a 5% difference in self-reported fun really corresponded precisely to a 5% difference in the level of fun that the player experienced? Of course not. But at the same time, I don't think anyone would argue that players can't tell for themselves if a game was fun or not. Our perceptions of our own mental states and experiences may be imperfect, but they're good enough for everyday purposes. If my friend says he's too cold, I don't need to hook him up to a skin temperature analyzer; I just turn up the thermostat.

HOW TO USE SELF-REPORT CORRECTLY

However, no matter how valuable self-report is as a research tool, the objections raised by psychologists are still valid. If we're going to use self-report, we must use it in ways that minimize its very real weaknesses.

First, self-reports cannot be taken at face value. If the players say a weapon was too weak, this is a statement of their opinion. It's not necessarily correct in an objective sense, but that's the way the player feels. When players rate a weapon as weak, we don't robotically take this as a mandate to increase weapon power. Maybe the weapon feedback is insufficient, maybe the players are using the wrong weapon on a particular enemy, or perhaps they missed the tutorial that would have taught them to use the weapon correctly. Player self-report is a symptom, not a diagnosis, and can be a powerful tool when understood and used in that context.

My favorite phrasing of this principle comes from author Neil Gaiman:

> *"Remember: when people tell you something's wrong or doesn't work for them, they are almost always right. When they tell you exactly what they think is wrong and how to fix it, they are almost always wrong."*

Secondly, we have objective data with which to sort and verify players' subjective feedback. Games are a particularly lucky medium when it comes to trying to understand our audience's experience. We have something that movies, books, and music don't: behavior. Our players aren't passively absorbing the game experience, they're participating in it. We don't just have a player's self-report about what weapon they liked best; we have their gameplay data as well. It's nice to know that players think the sniper rifle is the most powerful gun, but it's better to use gameplay data to tell the difference between someone who thinks it's overpowered because they got shot with it and someone who thinks it's overpowered because they used it.

Sorting subjective feedback according to objective telemetry is useful in other ways. It can be hard to pick a theme out of a hundred forum posts on a topic, but once those posts are sorted by other factors (skill rank, time spent playing, etc.) trends emerge very nicely from the chaos. The process can also be reversed, taking groups of similar comments and then looking at the telemetry for insights.

BACK TO BASICS

In some ways, self-report is a very primitive research method. It's one of the earliest tools used to study the mind, and like all early tools (fire, the wheel), it's simple and powerful. It's so fundamental that it's basically impossible not to use self-report when analyzing games, but so tainted that it can never be taken at face value. That's why researchers love it and hate it, use it and view it with deep suspicion. It's a primal part of our profession, a relic we cannot and should not outgrow. For all our pretensions and sophisticated methodologies, our PhD's and labs full of research equipment, there will always be a place and a time to just listen to our players.

CHAPTER 11
DESIGNERS ARE WEIRD

Game designers are not normal.

Okay, fine, no one in this industry is normal, but designers are even less normal than the rest of us. Like wine connoisseurs, designers experience hundreds or thousands of examples of the medium and are judging the current example on a very sophisticated palette. This platformer isn't just another game; it's a commentary on the nature of platformers, a response to four other games you've probably never heard of.

We actually want game designers to be abnormal. By definition, normal people don't make awesome games for the rest of us. Designers are supposed to be weirdos who think in special ways. But that means there are consistent distortions in how designers see the world that lead to standard problems in the resulting game design.

The job of a researcher is to help translate between designers and players, to make sure players have fun while experiencing whatever piece of five-dimensional performance art the designer thought they were making. We're not here to stop designer madness; we're here to help them make it work for the player. By making it work for the players, we make it work for the designer, too. If the game is received well, the designer gets to make more games.

This means embracing some things that designers value more than the rest of us, and letting those obsessions work for your game. Here are some examples, along with some advice on how to enable and channel them:

DIFFICULTY

Designers are dedicated gamers. This isn't a profession people end up in accidentally; it's a calling. They love games beyond all reason and will keep playing them past the point where most of us would quit in frustration.

To pick on a specific example, the first draft of one mission in the *Crimson Skies* Xbox game was insanely difficult because the designer had built it as a nice brisk challenge *for himself*. They eventually had to reduce the number of enemies in that mission by two-thirds before anyone else could reliably finish the mission.

Now, designers are not all necessarily world-class gamers. We made some challenge modes in *Destiny 1* that were too hard for anyone in the studio to complete. When they were released, some players completed them within hours. And challenges where game developers play online against their fans usually end with the developers being destroyed. But designers are generally more hardcore than average, if only because they're so passionate about games that they get a lot of practice hours.

The ultimate expression of this tendency is their love affair with "tough but fair" games. *Dark Souls* is designer catnip. I have yet to meet a designer who didn't drool over hardcore, punishing games like *Dark Souls, Elden Ring,* or *Cuphead.* They're great games, but they're also a distinct flavor that simply isn't enjoyable for many gamers.

How to handle this as a researcher:

Make them watch. The more designers watch, the more they empathize. If they watch a single clip showing a player failing at a particular point in their level, they can write that off as the player being bad. If they watch a longer section of gameplay, they'll have a chance to see the same issue multiple times, and they'll see the player succeeding as well. It's a lot harder to say "well, they're just bad at gaming" if the player has just been seen to handily defeat the rest of the level.

Make them set experience goals. These are things like "this mission should take 10 minutes," "players should die at least twice before beating the boss," etc. Designers often (incorrectly) write off subjective feedback, but it's much harder to argue with objective numbers. It's also worth noting that if they set the goals themselves, they're much more invested in them and they often set themselves a stricter target than you would.

Let them go crazy on the higher difficulty settings. *Halo* was designed primarily on the second hardest "Heroic" difficulty setting; according to the designers, that was the game's true form. The lower "Normal" and "Easy" modes were made by removing enemies from encounters and lowering the enemies' damage, rather than adding anything. In addition, we used the hardest "Legendary" difficulty setting as a release valve for the designers. Whenever anything was too hard for our participants, we just moved it to the higher difficulty settings and left it out of the mainstream experience. Of course, most players play on Normal or Easy, so these extra difficult parts of the game affect only a masochistic minority. But the designers got to feel that their vision has been achieved, so both parties were satisfied.

VARIETY

Designers don't want to stamp out the umpteenth variation of the same mission, they want to mix it up. They want to show their own twist on the formula and express who they are. If they didn't want to share their vision with the world, they'd be in a different line of work.

Examples of how this manifests are missions where the normal game mechanics are replaced by vehicles or alternate abilities, or where the player is forced to walk at half speed. (I'm looking at you, *Mass Effect*.) They're generally justified as "changes of pace" or "palette cleansers" in between more traditional missions. Swimming or water levels are also common examples of this, inducing groans and post-traumatic flashbacks in their victims. Just whisper the phrase "water temple" to any old school *Zelda* player and watch them flinch.

To a player, a game is like a movie: a perfect, unchanging artifact. To a designer, it's more like a gourmet meal: a transient experience where the interest is in the execution and variation. The creator proudly announces, "I made it with cilantro this time!" and the recipient responds with "gee thanks, you didn't need to do that..."

The thing is, players generally hate these variant sections. I've worked on dozens of games with missions where the normal game mechanics are suspended in favor of something novel. And in my entire career, none of those alternative missions ever tested as well as the standard gameplay. They almost always have the lowest scores and the most complaints of any section of the game.

The simple truth is that if the alternative mechanics were more fun than the core mechanics, we'd make them the main mechanics instead. Instead, what we get is something that is inevitably less polished and less fun than the core gameplay of the product, and then we force players to wade slowly through this swamp of novelty before they can proceed with the game they signed up to play.

How to handle this impulse as a researcher:

Make it easy. At a minimum, players should be able to progress through the novel content at the same rate they would with the normal game mechanics. You can always keep the altered mechanics but remove most of the challenges in that portion of the game.

Mass Effect 1's Mako vehicle sections are a good example of this solution. After months of playtesting where they tried different ways of making the Mako driving missions fun, the team gave up and just made those missions stupidly easy. They're still in the game and serve their original purpose as changes of pace, but they don't block progression anymore.

Make it optional. There's nothing wrong with having multiple ways to play the game. Achievements or bonus rewards that encourage players to play differently are great. Making stealth or pacifist playthroughs possible is wonderful and can extend the life of the game quite a bit for players that enjoy that sort of thing. Just let players opt out.

Make it short. If this part of the game is here for variety or a change of pace, then the length of the novelty doesn't matter. Make it five minutes of swimming, not fifty. We wanted to shake things up, we've done that, move on. Just ask the players how long that section felt, they'll tell you.

AMBIGUITY

In my experience, most players prefer to have clear goals. They want to know the correct thing to do, what they're supposed to be shooting at, and where they're supposed to go next. The most common purpose of playing a game is entertainment and feeling stupid or confused isn't generally fun. To players, the game is mostly about execution; Can they make the next jump or beat the next fight?

Designers, on the other hand, are way more comfortable with being lost or frustrated. They know that the game is arbitrary and that winning is less interesting than the experience of play. After all, their fundamental job as designers can be truthfully described as making things more complicated and confusing then they have to be.

A good example of this is waypoints. Game developers love the idea of removing waypoints to increase immersion. They build this big game with a vision of players wandering around, exploring, and discovering cool things. Then the players just walk straight to the waypoint, ignoring the scenery.

And to be fair, there are populations of players who like having to discover everything for themselves. There's just a lot fewer of them than designers like to believe. Like all the things on this list, it's not that no players like them, it's just that they're specialized tastes.

How to handle this as a researcher:

Let players speak for themselves. Give players a way to express their frustration during play. By the time the mission's over, they may have forgotten about being lost but that doesn't mean it didn't happen and won't make some players quit before they find the way forward. But if there's a way for players to indicate how they're feeling in the moment, you can identify and fix those temporary frustrations.

Set time limits. A few minutes of confusion is fine, an hour of confusion is torture. Work with the team to set goals for how long players should be stuck, then hold them to it. Worst case, investigate ways to nudge players in the right direction after a few minutes. For example, players in shooters generally move in the direction of the last enemy they saw, so in many *Halo* missions we would have a few easy enemies trickle in from the direction of the exit to pull players towards the way they should go.

TRANSIENCE

Designers are much less invested in a specific playthrough than the player is. They've played this game a million times during development, earned every piece of gear, then had to start over the next week. They care passionately about what they're creating, but it's also just one moment in a much larger process. They're not concerned that they weren't able to get the "best" ending on this playthrough, because they're going to play through the same mission another thirty times this week.

It is very much about the journey for designers, and many players (not all, but a substantial portion) feel that it's about the destination. That's one of the reasons why things that arbitrarily reset player progress tend to persist in games: Designers have experienced so many similar resets during development that they don't see the problem.

How to handle this as a researcher:

Make it realistic. The way designers play their games during development is not normal, but we can make what happens in our labs a little island of post-ship normality. Playthroughs in the lab should be as linear as possible, with gear and progress being gained and lost as normally as we can. Sure, we could use debug tools to teleport players around but that means players won't be as invested in their progress through the mission. Make players earn their progression in your tests, and they'll report the pain when that progress goes away.

Our job as researchers is to provide designers with the information necessary to be better designers. We're not trying to beat any of these tendencies down; we're trying to make sure that designers can still be designers but that players still have fun. We should not be imposing any constraints on designers that aren't surfacing in our testing. I may personally hate vehicle sections in games and know that they've been rated poorly in every game I've ever tested, but it's not my job to tell designers not to put them in. The most we can do is flag those sections as potential risks. They're not problems until players actually complain.

Once players do complain, however, the researcher must advocate fiercely for that complaint. The designer's right to swing their creativity ends at the tip of the player's nose. We want designers to be as free as possible while still making our players happy.

CHAPTER 12
THE NEED FOR SPEED

The development of *Halo 2* was quite troubled, and a lot of thought went into improving the process for *Halo 3*. For the studio, that meant creating a real production department and being more aggressive about controlling the scope of the game. For me as a researcher, I primarily wanted to avoid crunching. The final push to test *Halo 2* was probably the most intense crunch of my life, a months-long continuous push of working evenings and weekends. While I was proud of what I'd accomplished, I also never wanted to do anything like that again.

Rather than waiting for most of *Halo 3* to be completed and testing everything at the end, I was determined to get in there early and test at a steady, even pace. Accordingly, I started testing the game nearly a year earlier than I had with *Halo 2*. I engaged with the team steadily, running studies early and often, expecting that I could maintain the same controlled pace all the way to the end.

Instead, I ended up crunching anyway. Because many aspects of the game "came in hot," the pace of development increased sharply during the final months. New features were added, risky features were cut, and the game shifted radically from the version I'd tested. The result was that a lot of my earlier work had to be rerun, and I had to massively increase my pace of testing to match the pace of production.

Then on *Destiny*, the exact same thing happened. We started almost four years before ship, and we still ended up testing at a furious pace during the final months. Research is just fundamentally dependent on the rest of the development process, and there's only so much that can be done before everything comes together in an approximately final form.

Don't get me wrong: Working early was still great for the games. Early studies have their place, steering the ship of development through rocky early decisions. But there's never a case where early testing replaces later testing. It's additional work for an additional payoff and I should have budgeted it as such.

I'd also have been well served by making my testing faster and lighter. The research programs for *Halo* 2 and 3 have been held up as the premium version of user research, the epitome of high investment/high return. But they were also what has driven me to the conclusion that light and fast user research beats slow and thoughtful every time.

The single biggest shock to academic scientists when they move into the games industry is the speed. Most games research projects take weeks at most, not the usual months or even years of academic work. But even within the games industry, a lot of researchers try to slow things down, explicitly moving away from reactive work towards more slow-paced, strategic projects.

I tend to go the other way, pushing my teams to make their studies faster. I don't want to see a beautifully laid-out research timeline showing a multi-year schedule of evenly spaced studies. I'd rather hear "the team was worried about this topic yesterday so I'm putting it in the lab tomorrow." Planning and timelines have their place, but if I had to choose between good planning and good reaction times, I'd choose the later.

My reasoning has to do with the nature of the games industry, which is either dynamic (if you're feeling charitable) or chaotic (if you're not). Making games is hard, and it's extremely common for teams to radically alter their designs in the middle of development. Features change, storylines change, and sometimes even entire games get rebooted with a drastic change in art style or gameplay.

Researchers tend to be "downstream" of the rest of the development team. Every decision made by anyone in the studio will eventually manifest in the user experience, and a studio consists of dozens or hundreds of people making decisions all the time. The ability for research to react quickly to change is crucial, and we buy that agility by making our studies faster.

Here are some of the reasons why I love speed in research:

FAST IS THE SAME AS CHEAP IS THE SAME AS EASY

We can't run studies on short notice if they're expensive, or if the logistics of running them are too burdensome. By pushing for speed, we're also optimizing for many other virtues.

SPEED LETS YOU SAY "YES"

We want to encourage our dev partners to come to us with problems, so the fewer times we have to say no to them, the better. The faster we can answer each request, the more requests we can say "yes" to.

Fast/cheap/easy studies also let us say yes to marginal requests. Some topics that come to us are super important, and some are marginal. If studies are slow and expensive, we're forced to say no to everything below a certain level of importance. By reducing our investment per study, we allow ourselves the possibility of saying "yes" to more studies.

Those marginal studies might not be all that impactful in themselves, but they can lead to more powerful collaborations down the road. Having the spare resources to build up relationships is incredibly valuable, even if the extra studies themselves are not.

SPEED ALLOWS ITERATION

Running studies faster means that we can test the same piece of the game multiple times. This is great for iterating on both the game and the research process.

For the game, retesting the same content means that you can both confirm the problems found in the earlier study have been fixed and find new problems that were hidden under the old ones. Similarly, we can iteratively improve the study design. I've never run a perfect study, and it's common to realize after a study is over that there's an additional question we should have asked or that there's a different sequence of gameplay that would have created a clearer picture of the problem. The more versions of a study, the more it improves.

SPEED ALLOWS EXPERIMENTATION

The slower it is to run a study, the more conservative we have to be about study design. If we only get one shot at a particular topic, we have to pick the way of approaching it that has the highest guarantee of success. We might not have the time or the budget to do it again if something goes wrong.

In a world where studies are cheap and plentiful, we have room to try radical things. In the best case, we'll get better data than we would have with a more conventional design. Worst case, we just run it again with a more proven design, because…

SPEED ALLOWS RECOVERY FROM MISTAKES

Cheap fast studies can be rerun quickly. Not just from our own mistakes, but from malfunctioning software, bad participants, unexpected fire drills, etc. No matter how careful our preparations, some studies will fail. It's never fun to blow a study but wasting a few days of work is much less painful than wasting weeks of work. Also, if our setup time for a new study is fast enough, we might even be able to hit the original delivery date for the results. Saying "we'll just rerun this tomorrow" is an amazing luxury.

SPEED ALLOWS US TO SCALE OUR INVESTMENT

In a perfect world, a researcher and their dev partners care an equal amount about each study. But in reality, there is a certain minimum of work involved in each study for the researcher, due to the nature of recruiting, lab set up, etc. Optimizing our research processes for speed reduces that minimum investment. By making each study require less work, we can invest in smaller increments, giving each topic exactly as much love as it deserves.

SPEED ALLOWS US TO TOUCH MORE OF THE GAME

We all have a limited number of researcher-hours we can devote to a given game. That means we'll inevitably have to make a prioritized list of topics we want to test, and we'll never make it all the way to the bottom. In every game I've shipped, there are areas that we made a conscious decision not to test. It might be endgame content that most players won't reach, obscure game modes that most players don't know about, or just parts of the game world off the beaten path. It sucks to know those aspects of the game will have problems we could have found and fixed if we'd had time.

However, being able to run more studies in the same amount of time means we can reach further down the list. We'll never reach the bottom, but we can at least do basic coverage of a wider swath of the game, with multiple passes on the key areas.

Fast studies don't just happen. It takes a highly developed foundation to run a real playtest on short notice. Here's some of the attributes that enable my research teams to run quick, responsive studies.

VERTICAL INTEGRATION

I'm a strong believer in the idea that researchers should own their participant recruiting and labs. You can't be fast if you're waiting on someone else to get you participants or for a shared lab space to be free. The research team should be a self-contained unit, with as few external dependencies as possible. This is a hassle but pays off in speed and flexibility. Owning your own systems means you control the entire process and can make it run on your schedule to your own specifications.

BUILD RELATIONSHIPS AHEAD OF TIME

The better we and our partners understand each other before the study idea comes up, the faster and smoother the study will go. The more we've worked together, the fewer technical hurdles we'll encounter, and the fewer review iterations are required. The real killer for speed is waiting for other people, so the more in sync everyone is, the less waiting around will need to happen on any given study.

RUN THROWAWAY STUDIES TO WARM THE PIPELINE

This is one way to make sure people are in sync: Recognizing that our first study on any game is going to be wasted. Recursively, our first study on any individual topic inside the game is likely to be wasted. This is both because we haven't built up the trust for the first studies to be truly effective, but also because we don't know how to optimize our research for this game or feature yet. It'll turn out that the study needs to be run in a particular order, or that participants need to warm up in one mode before trying another. Some of these things can be deduced ahead of time, but a lot of them must be discovered through hard experience in the lab. Building a throwaway first study can, ironically, give that study more purpose—because every study teaches us how to run better studies. We learn what works and what doesn't through experience. It's easier and cheaper to do that with simple, low-stakes studies, with proper expectations. The more substantial studies will flow faster and easier if all the little problems have been sanded out ahead of time.

KEEP IT SIMPLE.

Remember, the core of this profession is getting a real player to play the game while designers watch. That is a very simple mandate, and while we can add on all sorts of elaborations to our studies, they're not actually required. It's almost always possible to speed up the research cycle by throwing the fancy stuff overboard.

The reason there can be so much fancy stuff to begin with is the natural way studies get more sophisticated over time. Procedures and habits accumulate. We add a section to the post-study questionnaire about weapon balance, and it's easier just to leave it in for the next study. The players have to create characters for each playtest, so we keep asking about character creation. We add an extra pre-study check-in meeting with the stakeholders to make sure everyone's happy and we won't have that one argument again.

We don't even notice this feature creep because we're getting so much better at running the study. Then one day, we find ourselves saying "We can't do this study because we don't have time"—because we're judging the time it takes to run the elaborate version, not the time for the minimalist version. The pressure of speed is a gift, pushing us towards parsimony and elegance.

KEEP THE SCOPE TIGHT

No individual study solves everything. We never do just one study on a game, so our goal should never be testing the entire game all in one shot. We just want to fix the maximum number of issues before release, and the most efficient way to do that is a steady stream of lightweight studies. Don't feel the need to add every possible game mode and task to every study. Keep it tightly focused on the earliest, most important issues.

DON'T FIND MORE PROBLEMS THAN YOU CAN FIX.

It's a brutal truth that development teams only have a limited amount of bandwidth and resources to respond to any given study. In a perfect world, a study finds the same number of issues that the team will fix. While it's true some smaller issues will slip by, they're exactly that: smaller issues. Almost any study will find the major issues, and those larger issues will be the ones that get prioritized anyway.

PRIORITIZE FINDING RESULTS THAT THE TEAM CARES ABOUT

The results of a study should be presented as a list of findings sorted in order of importance to the players and the design team. This goes back to the need to build relationships ahead of time. The better we know what the team cares about and can act on, the more focused our analysis can be.

STANDARDIZE EVERYTHING

The most precious resource in any research study is the researcher's attention. Standardizing aspects of the study frees up our minds. Standardization also lets researchers make fewer mistakes while operating at high speed. If we only have a short time to choose a participant profile, for example, starting from an existing profile template means all the major concerns are laid out visibly in front of us. Having checklists for procedures also supports speed and reduces the odds of mistakes.

GET THE TEAM TO WATCH

As I've said multiple times in this book, the best data collection tool in any study is the eye of the designer. The person who made the thing is a better judge of whether it's working as intended than anyone else.

When it comes to keeping studies fast, making the team watch means that 90% of your impact is finished by the end of the study. Yes, we'll want to run some analysis and create a report for posterity, but the simple act of watching the study creates most of the impact. We can't fall so in love with our own analytical brilliance that we undervalue the immense contribution of the rest of the team. Our analysis is optional; the team's is not.

There's also nothing wrong with running a study with no reporting if we're under sufficient time pressure. Bring in the players, let the team observe, have a quick debrief with them afterwards, and we're done. Sure, such tests are crude blunt instruments compared to what can be done with a thoughtful in-depth analysis. That's fine; hammers and mallets are still as useful today as they were a thousand years ago. Any valid study is better than no study.

KEEP THE PIPELINE CLEAR

In true Kanban style, each research study should be completed and clear before the next study begins. The main reason a new study can't start right now is that the researcher is busy. Therefore, being responsive means that we need to get the researcher un-busy as soon as possible after they commit to a study. Being fast with the current study in turn enables the next study to be fast.

DON'T RUN STUDIES WE DON'T HAVE TO

A corollary to moving studies through the pipeline as quickly as possible is to avoid filling the pipeline with dud studies. Whatever study we're running now must be more valuable than whatever else we could be doing with the time. Ideally, our research team should always be busy, but we should only have just enough of a backlog to stay busy. A long backlog means we're cluttering up our future with studies that aren't important enough to run right now and which probably will turn out to be less important than requests that will arise later.

CREATE STRATEGIC RESOURCES TO DRAW ON

Creating a study from scratch is a slow process, so a smart researcher will have done as much of the work as they can ahead of time. Studies should be built out of standard parts, built during downtimes in the production cycle. For example, having templates for all the various aspects of a study can save a lot of time. Similarly, a research team can build strategic resources like player segmentations, previously recruited pools of different types of participants, or libraries of prevetted questions. Like maintaining your own labs, these sorts of resources take quite a bit of up-front work to build, but the result is a much more agile process in the moment.

If we believe that research is a good thing for the product, then being able to do more research is better. Speed lets us execute more studies, cheaper, easier, and on time. Speed forces us to be better researchers, focused on getting exactly the results that matter most as efficiently as possible.

Being a fast and agile researcher feels a bit like being a superhero—but more along the lines of Batman than Superman. Fast studies come from monomaniacal focus, preparation, and self-discipline. It's not a comfortable process, but it means that we can be the hero our developers need.

CHAPTER 13
THE CARE AND FEEDING OF RESEARCH PARTICIPANTS

A good researcher maintains two simultaneous contradictory mindsets about their participants. On one hand, our participants are unique and beautiful individuals who have volunteered to help us make a better game and they're deserving of our respect and gratitude. We have an absolute, ironclad obligation to make sure they are safe, comfortable, and that they have the most pleasant experience in our lab that we can arrange.

On the other hand, our participants are also walking bags of data to be squeezed as hard and efficiently as possible. As researchers, we're not there to be community managers or ambassadors. We're trying to collect as much clean data as possible as quickly as possible, and to get the information our designers need in time for them to act.

Those principles need to exist in perfect balance in a researcher's mind, guiding every decision we make. Even with the most meticulously designed study plan in the world there are always decisions that need to be made in the moment. The best way to make sure those on-the-fly decisions are correct is to have a small set of principles to compare against the current situation.

Here are some core principles to making sure things run as smoothly as possible:

SET EXPECTATIONS

While this may be the researcher's thousandth usability session, it's likely to be the participant's first. The better we can lay out what's going to happen and what the participant's role will be, the more comfortable they'll be. This can start from the first email or phone contact with the participant and continues right up until they leave the building. Most researchers start a session with a prepared speech that lays out what's coming up.

MAKE SURE THEY KNOW THEIR RIGHTS

Participants must be told they can take breaks or leave whenever they need to. You can ask that they try to time their breaks to happen in between multiplayer matches or some other natural stopping point, but you're not there to be a hall monitor. Worst case, the session can be written off and the data discarded. The people in your study are more important than the data.

Because participants always think they're the ones being tested, they will try to push past levels of frustration and unhappiness that would normally cause them to quit playing at home. There's a certain level of self-care that people perform in their own environments that they won't replicate in a lab setting when someone is watching them. (The infamous Milgram experiment is a particularly horrible example of this effect.) As the person who owns the room, you're responsible for maintaining awareness of the participant experience and offering them a way out when it gets too rough. Participants never remember their rights on their own, which means you must remember for them and prompt them to take advantage of those rights.

ASSURE THEM THAT THEY'RE NOT BEING TESTED

The simple truth is, we're not testing the participants; we're testing the game. Errors or failures by the participant truly are the fault of the game. The researcher needs to make this clear to the participants, letting them know that they can relax and play normally—and that their normal gameplay and natural reactions are exactly what the process needs. Unfortunately, no participant will ever believe you when you tell them this. They always, always think they're the one on trial. Remember this and be kind.

BE PERSONABLE, NOT PERSONAL

It's vital that participants feel as comfortable and relaxed as they can during a study. We're trying to simulate how they'd feel when playing at home, after all. Don't be afraid to start a study with a little small talk about their drive in to the studio, the weather, recent movies, whatever. Smile. This is just one more study for you, but for them it's a strange and potentially nerve-wracking experience combining the awesomeness of meeting a celebrity with the scrutiny of a trip to the dentist. Be kind, be friendly, help them to relax and play normally.

At the same time, it's also important to set boundaries. You're not there to be their friend; you're there to get data. Don't share your last name or too much about the studio or the research team. You don't want to contaminate their opinions or their feedback. We're here to get information out of them, not to put information in.

NEVER LAUGH AT THEM

If the researcher laughs at the participant, you might as well send them home. Players are nervous enough in the lab to begin with, and extremely sensitive to any sign they're doing things wrong. It's fine to laugh *with* the participant if something funny happens, but they themselves can never, ever be the joke. If you laugh *at* them, the session is over. You don't have an engaged participant anymore, just someone who's deliberately under-reacting to avoid embarrassment.

TRAIN YOUR TEAM

Running a live games research study is an overwhelming experience, like simultaneously working as a wedding planner and a surgeon. There are a million things going on and a fair proportion of them will be going wrong at any given time. Participants will be having micro-crises, hardware will be breaking, and the game build won't launch when it's supposed to.

Part of making sure participants have a good experience is making sure the research team is fully prepared. Having good stock answers to common questions and a set of troubleshooting escalation procedures established ahead of time means things are more likely to be handled the right way in the middle of the chaos.

This is particularly important when doing any research involving minors. Some normal testing practices (such as not allowing non-staff observers) obviously don't apply when the participant is a child. Tests with kids also tend to inspire more challenges, like the parent bringing the siblings along, and the team needs to know in advance how they're going to handle things.

PROTECT YOUR TEAM

The players who show up to playtests are fans, but it's only a small step from "dedicated fan" to "crazed stalker." Don't share last names, where people live, what they do outside of work, or anything about studio schedules or procedures. Be friendly, but vague. Participants should come out of the test knowing nothing more about the research team than "they were nice to me."

Special care needs to be taken to protect female researchers. It's an unfortunate truth that the gamer community includes a lot of poorly socialized men and some of those have trouble telling the difference between a woman being pleasantly professional and one who's flirting. Both the female researchers and their male colleagues need to be careful not to mention last names or any clues that might aid a participant in finding a female researcher online after the study.

TAKE AWAY THEIR PHONES

I know, I know, in the modern age this seems like amputating a limb, but participant phones are an unacceptable security risk in the lab. The internet has plenty of anonymous rumors about any popular game, so a few more unsubstantiated statements from people who claim to have been playtesters are unlikely to get much traction. But a leak with accompanying pictures is a very different matter. Because every phone is also a camera these days, you need to treat every phone as an unacceptable leak risk.

Sometimes, participants do have legitimate reasons for needing to check their phones during a study or even to be ready to take a call. In those cases, ask if it's sufficient for a researcher to hold the phone for them, ready to let them know if it rings.

MAKE SURE YOU HAVE ENOUGH STAFF ON HAND

Participants should never be left unattended, which means that it's often necessary to have multiple researchers present for a study. A general rule of thumb is a minimum of two researchers for any study, with at least one researcher per five participants for larger studies.

This is particularly true at the start of any given study session. If anything is going to go wrong, it'll happen early. That's when you'll discover that the game's servers are offline on Tuesdays, that a participant has a behavioral issue, or that someone misplaced all the headphones. And when those things go wrong, it's great to have a lot of extra assistants on hand to get everything sorted out.

The tricky part is getting everyone in their seats and in the groove. Once they're playing and giving feedback in the appropriate rhythm, the study will be smooth sailing. Most of the helpers can go back to their desks and leave the study in the hands of just two people. I say a minimum of two because the participants can't be left alone with the game, lest someone run off with the testing PC or start taking pictures of the screen, and researchers do need to be able to leave the lab for bathroom breaks, etc.

HAMMER THE NDA

Non-disclosure agreements are one of the fundamentals of the user research process. Every participant that comes into the lab from outside signs one, and they are a real, legally binding document that can be prosecuted in court if necessary. However, participants often treat them like software EULAs or terms of service: something they sign and forget. Since participants don't usually take a copy away with them, they can sometimes forget the exact terms of what they signed.

It's important to remind participants about the NDA at every opportunity. Remind them in the beginning, at the end, when you say goodbye at the door. These reminders don't have to be accusatory or lecturing. In fact, I've had my best results when framing it as "you're going to see something so cool we have to swear you to secrecy." The best way to get people to obey the NDA is to emphasize that the secrecy is necessary if we're going to run these sorts of pre-release studies. If the team doesn't believe the game will remain confidential, they won't allow the study to take place and we'll end up shipping a worse game.

THANK THEM AND GIVE THEM A GIFT

Participants are not employees, but they are doing something that directly benefits the game. They deserve to walk away with something for their time. Generally, we call this a "gratuity" and it's most commonly a gift card or even a cash payment on the order of $50 to $100 for a short session or up to $200 for a longer playtest. I personally think it's important that they also leave the studio with a physical gift whenever possible. It's a bit of a hassle maintaining an inventory of t-shirts in multiple sizes or a giant pile of posters, but offering nothing but money makes the study feel too much like a purely mercenary transaction. The core of any study is making the game better through player feedback, and you want players to really believe that. If they're just hanging out in the lab for an hour for their fifty bucks, they're more likely to not take the study seriously (leading to bad data) or not take the NDA seriously (leading to leaks).

If people were simple, we wouldn't need to do these sorts of studies in the first place. While the design and output of a study might look like science, running the study itself looks more like politics: an endless series of compromises trying to satisfy conflicting goals.

Our participants are simultaneously real people with feelings and tools to improve the game. While these two attitudes towards participants do create some tension, fundamentally both are necessary. We must respect our participants if we want to get good data out of them and getting good data in turn is what makes all the participants' efforts worthwhile. Players want to be part of the process of making a better game, and we owe it to them to both treat them well and make their time count.

CHAPTER 14
REALISM IN RESEARCH

There's a common belief that a user research study needs to simulate natural play to be meaningful. Some researchers turn their labs into elaborate "living room simulators," complete with potted plants and comfy couches, in an attempt to make the environment as homelike as possible. Other researchers argue against research methods that disrupt the normal play experience, such as asking a participant to think out loud or having them stop to answer a questionnaire while playing.

These objections come from a mistaken notion of what we're trying to do in the lab. While it's true that we're trying to find the problems that would disrupt the normal play experience, that doesn't mean that the method used to find those problems has to look anything like how we play at home. Medical x-ray imaging is profoundly unnatural, but the problems it finds are just as real outside of the hospital. To frame it more positively, think of putting a game through a research study like going to the gym. Lifting a barbell repeatedly or contorting in a Nautilus machine don't closely resemble movements of everyday life, but they are intended to build muscles that still benefit you in real world situations. The circumstances in which we detect a weakness don't necessarily have anything to do with how those things impact the real player experience.

For example, we generally don't let players use outside resources to solve problems they encounter in the lab, even though that's something that might happen in a "normal" home environment. Just because at-home players can access FAQ websites or hand the controller to their more adept sibling to get past a frustrating part of the game doesn't mean that frustration wasn't real or that it wouldn't cost the game a meaningful fraction of its players who can't or won't dip into outside resources. Problems might be more prominent in the lab, but they're still real problems.

REALITY IS INEFFICIENT

Non-naturalistic procedures in the lab have other benefits as well. Lab studies often benefit from larger sample sizes, which is difficult to do if each play session is an artisanal recreation of the home experience. Running twenty players through the first hour of a game one at a time could take a full work week just for data collection. In contrast, if all twenty players play simultaneously, the study can be done in an afternoon. Sure, having a large group of people play side by side isn't a normal real-world experience, but the efficiency gains are generally considered to be worth it.

By reducing unnecessary realism, we make studies cheaper, faster, and more efficient. Even if we assume that naturalistic play makes the study results better, non-naturalistic studies may still result in more net benefits for the game. If a naturalistic research study produces a set of data that's better but takes twice as long to collect, a researcher might still produce a better impact on the game by running two less naturalistic studies. In the end, the job of the researcher isn't to produce optimal individual studies, it's to create the most positive research impact on the final game.

A CASE STUDY IN UNREALITY

When we were playtesting *Halo* campaigns, we faced the dilemma that the story was simply too long for most players to reasonably complete in a single day, or even in full weekend of playtesting. While we could get players to come to our lab for both Saturday and Sunday, lunch breaks and other logistical concerns meant that we couldn't get more than ten hours of gameplay from any individual. Since the campaign were generally longer than that, we were faced with either not testing the end of the campaign (scary) or finding a different, less realistic method for getting that data. Bringing people back for a third day of testing was possible but started to run into issues of selection bias. Lots of people are willing to come play games for one weekend, but a third day meant they'd probably either be skipping a day of work or coming back the next weekend. Either option would make the studies take longer and bias them towards ultra-hardcore players.

Instead, we opted to skip some players ahead. All participants played the first few hours of the game, and then a random sample were moved several missions later in the game, given a short story synopsis of the missions they jumped over and allowed to finish the game as normal. Because both groups played some of the same later missions, we could compare how the two groups played those missions and reassure ourselves that the jump hadn't resulted in a drastically different experience for the two groups.

Mission	Group 1	Group 2
1	Played	Played
2	Played	Played
3	Played	Skipped
4	Played	Skipped
5	Played	Played
6	Played	Played
7	Didn't reach	Played
8	Didn't reach	Played

How skipping some players ahead produces better campaign coverage

This solution would not necessarily work for every type of game. In a traditional FPS campaign, missions in the middle of the game can be somewhat interchangeable. In a game like *Portal*, where the player is expected to learn new mechanics frequently throughout the game and then use those mechanics in combination in later levels, skipping would have compromised the experience. But in this case, thoughtfully deviating from the naturalistic experience allowed us to learn things we wouldn't have otherwise.

KEEPING IT REAL

All that said, realism is still sometimes a good idea, even if it's not a strict requirement. As discussed earlier, the primary limiting factor for most research is how much the development team believes in the results. Realism can be a useful tool in making our results believable and means that we have to spend less time defending and explaining our methods to non-researchers. In general, when working with a new design team, it's best to start with more naturalistic methods and work up from there as trust is built.

Realism is always a useful default, and researchers should be thoughtful about how we translate the normal game experience in the lab. In testing the Xbox karaoke game *Lips*, researchers discovered that one aspect of the naturalistic karaoke experience was non-negotiable: alcohol. It turned out that singing karaoke stone cold sober in a lab setting was so alien to the spirit of the activity that participants just couldn't do it. Thankfully, the studio had a liquor license and was able to provide the players with the necessary refreshments to restore the natural experience.

This is also a good argument for doing home visits with players. A lot of what happens in a normal home game session is external to both the game and the player. People may be playing in a shared common room and have to mute the sound periodically, or they might have a page of hints open on a second screen or hand off the controller to a family member to get past a hard boss fight. Even if there's perfect logging of what's happening in-game, huge aspects of the experience can be unknown unless seen in the natural gaming environment.

A great example of this is the early testing on Microsoft's Kinect vision system. The system generally did best when there was a large clear space in front of the television, more space than was available in many homes. The researchers who worked on Kinect conducted home visits to watch players unpack and set up the device (the "out-of-box experience"). The setup tutorial would ask players to step farther back from the screen, but their couches would be in the way. A game design team sitting in their nice conference room might assume that the logical response to this would be to shift the couch back to create a larger play area. In fact, what the researchers observed is that the players would step up onto their couch, creating the distance without having to move heavy furniture. This never would have happened in a laboratory setting where the furniture was purchased and placed with the Kinect in mind.

CHOOSING WHEN TO BREAK THE RULES

The question isn't "should our research be realistic?" The question is "how does our testing methodology help or harm what we're trying to learn in this case?" Sometimes we can conveniently abstract a part of the game to study it, and other times taking a game out of context compromises the experience. This is part of why researchers have jobs: not just to execute formulaic studies but to make thoughtful decisions about how and when to break the rules.

CHAPTER 15
THE BEST DATA IS THE DATA YOU HAD ALL ALONG

Once a research question arises, regardless of where it comes from, our job is to come up with an answer. There are three basic kinds of data we can tap into to answer the question:

1. Data we already have
2. Data we can get without leaving our desks
3. Data generated from a new study

Let's go through each of them in turn:

The best data is data you already have. Ideally, the research team has been busy doing things all this time and has a project that's at least slightly relevant to the current question. It might not be a direct hit, but it's close enough. Someone might ask "What's the most fun mount in the game?" and while you might not have satisfaction data for the mounts, you might have usage data. Sure, "mount that gets used the most when people have other options" isn't the same thing as "mount that people like the most," but it's close enough for many purposes.

You lose nothing by offering your team what's already on hand. Worst case, they say that's not quite right and you have to do the more in-depth research project you would have otherwise. Best case, you're a magician who solved their problem instantly.

This is also why it's worth doing regular player surveys and standardized playtests. Having a robust set of reasonably recent information is an amazing resource. Even if you didn't precisely ask the question they're interested in, having a pile of general-purpose recent data on hand is a great starting place for a more thorough investigation. If you're asked "why are people quitting this week", being able to pull the last general survey and look at how the respondents' answers correlate with their retention rate is a great first approximation.

Another good example of this kind of ready-to-hand data is achievement data. Compared to real gameplay logging, achievements are blunt instruments, being just binary has it/doesn't have it values. But each achievement secretly encodes a lot more information. In the bad old days of the early 2000s, when game logging was relatively primitive, we used achievements for a lot of different things. Most of the early *Halo* data analysis was built on achievements rather than gameplay data, just because that's what was easily available. The pattern of achievements earned by a player can easily serve as a fingerprint.

It's also worth noting that the specific data that we're asked for isn't always the most relevant to the decision the person who requested the data is trying to make. The data you have on hand might actually be a better answer than what they asked for.

The second-best kind of data is the kind you can get without leaving your desk. I don't necessarily mean literally at your desk; I'm referring here to data you can get without scheduling a new lab study. This includes deeper analytics work, surveys, and tacking extra questions onto upcoming studies.

Putting together this sort of data is harder than just pulling something that already exists off the shelf, but it does bypass a lot of the complications that slow down creating new data from scratch. It involves fewer moving parts than creating new studies, and often can be done asynchronously, in whatever pieces of time are free in between meetings and existing studies. It also doesn't take any scarce resources like lab time or budget.

This data you can gather from your desk is a midpoint between our two other categories, in both speed and targeting. It's slower than just tapping into existing data, but it's certainly faster than running a new study. It's also more on-point than existing data, but not as tightly focused as new data. For example, if you tag an extra section onto a preplanned survey, you're still limited to the same recipients as that survey. Similarly, digging through existing analytics data can provide something useful ("30% of players have gotten a kill with a grenade launcher") without being precisely what the designer wanted ("How many players have ever picked up a grenade launcher?").

The worst data is new data you have to go out and create. Don't misunderstand me, I love running studies. Nothing makes me happier than a day in the lab. But studies are slow, even under the best circumstances. They require scheduling, booking the lab and recruiting participants. They also demand a researcher's full attention for days at a time, even under the best circumstances.

The joy of new data, of course, is that it can be perfectly designed around the current research topic. You can recruit exactly the right participants, ask them precisely the right questions, and hand the team the best possible answer. This is the high-end service with all the bells and whistles, appropriate for the highest priority problems.

There is also an analytics equivalent here: adding new logging to the game to answer the question. While this is often less total work than a lab study, it generally must go through other departments (engineering to create the logs, QA to validate them, etc.) and there can be a delay of weeks or months before the new logging makes it into the live game.

One additional note is that a good researcher thinks ahead when they run their studies, with an eye towards a future where their new data might fall into the other two categories. A good study is one that isn't too tightly focused, that collects a little more data than you need, just in case. You might only care about players' opinions of the game's weapons right now, but you might as well ask them about the other equipment while you're at it. The extra data might save you from having to run another study later.

This is one of the differences between academic and industry research. An academic study generally starts with a hypothesis and then assembles exactly the data needed to prove/disprove that hypothesis. But in industry, we're doing something much fuzzier and holistic. Think of it like taking a photograph of a larger area than you really need, with the intention of cropping down to a targeted area for the final version but also saving the complete picture.

Similarly, making a study backwards compatible can also extend its potential usefulness. If you can reasonably use the same kind of player as an earlier study to test a new part of the game or retest the same mission with a different population, you extend your body of insights by allowing between-study comparisons. If a study is too tightly optimized for the current need, it can break compatibility with other studies.

Every study should always have some space for just letting the user talk or make open comments. Having a generic "what's one thing you'd change about the game" question in a survey, for example, might or might not be relevant to the current goal of the survey, but it provides an interesting cross-check on the rest of the results and often proves to be a useful resource later. Even a question like "what was your favorite moment when playing today?" can create opportunities for data you didn't know you needed.

Now, one might look at this philosophy and think that it's hostile to the rest of the team, focusing on giving them leftovers whenever possible. But in practice, the result is happier partners. They don't care if it's new data or old or even perfect; they just want the answers necessary to build the right thing. Being smart about reusing prior work and extending planned work instead of adding new work results in more throughput for our partners. Remember, they're operating most of the time in a complete information vacuum. Anything we can do for them is an improvement and doing it fast and cheap means we can do more of it. If we're somewhat stingy in our support of any specific request, we can answer more requests in total. That makes all our designers happier.

PART THREE
COMMUNICATION

CHAPTER 16
BRING THE PAIN

One day during the big production crunch for *Halo 3*, I had a meeting with the design team. As the meeting's attendees trickled in and sat down, I put on a video from the previous day's playtest, just to give people something to watch while they waited for the last few stragglers to arrive.

The player in the video was driving a Warthog vehicle full speed towards the last enemy in the encounter, hoping to ram them. They succeeded in splattering the last enemy but had too much momentum to stop themselves from flying off a cliff afterwards. In midair, the "Checkpoint Reached" message appeared just as they fell to their death. The player then immediately respawned at the checkpoint in mid-air and fell to their death again. This cycled four or five more times as the design team watched, then one of them said the very first words that had been spoken in the meeting:

"We'll fix that."

The end goal of games user research is to reduce the amount of pain users experience when playing the game after release. We do this by simulating that pain in the lab. A playtest that is too easy on the players and designers is a wasted playtest. A good usability study should be hard on everyone involved.

This may seem overly melodramatic, but it's more accurate than not. Good research isn't just true, it's *motivational*. There are a lot of other things that designers need and want to be doing besides reacting to this set of results. They already have a giant backlog of tasks, a bunch of pet projects they want to squeeze into the schedule, and they'd really like to go home at some point…

Research results must be so powerful that the designers and engineers and artists will put aside everything else they could be doing and dig into fixing the problems we've uncovered. The best way to do that is to show how much pain the problems are causing the players. The entire point of being a game designer is to make players happy by creating an enjoyable experience. The most motivating thing a designer can see is a player not having fun while playing their content.

Here are some of the ways I've been able to create motivation with data:

MAKE THEM WATCH

Reports and videos are great, but there is no substitute for direct personal viewing. I move heaven and earth to get my developers into the lab to see things like that cliff-dive "checkpoint" loop for themselves. Designers seeing problems with their own eyes is more convincing than anything I can say.

My designers are also better at picking up problems with gameplay than I am; that's why they're designers. The same study will find more and better issues with the game by having a designer present to see things for themselves. Every piece of design has lots of subtle bits of intent that the designer could never put into words, but it's all contained in their mental image of how a playthrough of their content will go. The only real way for those smaller intents to be verified is to have designers personally observe a player.

Also, to put it bluntly: If the study is not important enough for the team to attend at least one session, it's not important enough for me to run. That sounds harsh, but they're not invested enough to show up, they're unlikely to act on the results anyway.

There's also magic in making designers slow down and experience the user pain in real time. Designers reading a report or watching a video can skip ahead, even when they agree that what they're seeing is a problem. Reality can't be skipped; they have to stand there and empathize with every agonizing second.

HUMANIZE THE DATA

It's a perverse truth of user research that the most reliable data we generate (metrics, quantitative ratings, etc.) is the least persuasive, while the most subjective (individual stories, facial expressions, etc.) can be the most powerful. While the job of a researcher is to understand the objective truth, there's nothing that says I can't use more persuasive tools to add texture to objective data.

Whenever possible, quantitative data should be accompanied by a matching piece of qualitative data: a comment, a screenshot, a video, a sound bite, etc. I don't let the squishy stuff drive the issues, but instead use it to put flesh on the numerical bones. (This is also a good sanity check for me. If I can't find a quote or a snippet of video to support a statistic, I'm probably looking at the wrong statistic.)

Video is great, particularly if the designer can just watch the highlight reel. However, it's still not quite as good as watching in person, because when watching a recording designers can skip ahead, fast forward, glance over to their email on the other monitor, etc.

This prevents a lot of quibbling about specific numbers. Reporting that someone struggled to open a door for 30 seconds might be ambiguous but showing a video of their expression while they do it is a lot more convincing than the amount of time elapsed.

This isn't just true for negatives. Seeing a player smiling or laughing while playing their content is the most powerful reward a developer can have. Everything I'm talking about in this chapter can also be used to drive home positive points—and including human moments undercuts any accusations that the researcher is biasing the results in either direction. I could be making up a number, but I can't fake a video clip.

USE THE UNHOLY POWER OF STORIES

In the *Halo 3* Warthog example earlier, I used a recording of a one-off incident to convince the design team to change something. Humans respond to stories, even when those stories are not representative of the larger picture. The famous quote about the plural of "anecdote" not being "data" is true, but people are still wired to relate to each other in terms of stories. A smart researcher selectively deploys stories to support the objective statistical findings. This doesn't mean anecdotes should be used on their own. But done the right way, used in conjunction with real analysis and numbers, representing the reality of those findings, they provide excellent support.

ALLOW USERS TO KEEP FAILING

When players are struggling at a particular point in the game, it's always tempting to be compassionate and help the player past the trouble spot. Logically, this shouldn't matter. The participant has clearly hit a wall and we're wasting study time that could be used to detect another issue. Five deaths at the same checkpoint are enough to prove the problem, right?

Not necessarily. It's not enough that the evidence proves the problem to an objective observer; it must be convincing to the specific person who created the problem. I can't tell you how many times a designer has said to me "they would have gotten it in another minute or two," or acknowledged the problem but never actually made any fixes. Designers aren't objective in evaluating their own content any more than parents objectively assess their own children. The evidence must be completely undeniable by anyone with a shred of integrity.

So, it's vital that researchers are not too quick to declare a fail. We can't pull our punches. If we stop once the situation is convincing to us personally, we're probably stopping too soon. We must wait until it's overwhelming, until there's no way any sane person could deny the problem. Every player death, every frustrated sigh… they're all ammunition for the potential fight I'm going to have with the designers after the study. I can't limit my ammo supply. I have to let the users fail now to create the leverage I need to make sure no one else goes through this again.

OK so once we've run the study and brought the pain, what next? Ideally, the designers see the evidence and go immediately back to their desks to fix the issues. Unfortunately, often developers will make excuses when confronted with user pain. They're facing something uncomfortable, and it's natural for them to push back, to defend themselves. It's the researcher's job to hold them accountable, for their own good and for the good of the players.

Here are some of the most common ways designers try to deflect research findings and the best counterarguments we can use to drive the findings home:

"IT WAS SELF-INFLICTED."

Designers will often argue that the user did this to themselves. The level already has tons of training and cues, and it's not the designer's fault that the player deliberately did things the hard way. The counterargument is that nothing is self-inflicted in a game. We built the world, we built the rules, and it's all our responsibility.

At best, we should make sure the user can't do that to themselves. At worst, we should have an easy recovery path. For example, say the player deleted a key item needed for the quest and was stuck for ten minutes. Yes, that was dumb of them, but why should it even be possible to do that? Can we have the quest-giver provide a replacement on demand? Does the item need to be in the game at all? There's lots of ways that a good designer can let users recover from their own mistakes.

"THIS PARTICIPANT IS A BAD PLAYER."

Half of all players are going to be below average, and some are far below average. Designers will push back saying that what they're being shown doesn't reflect the average experience, and that modifying the design to help this player would devalue the experience for normal players.

Our response should be that even bad players have a right to enjoy the game. A game should fail gracefully, letting poor players progress slowly and finish at a bare minimum. Sure, there are always side missions or achievements meant for experts, but the central path of the experience should be achievable for anyone. Even the very worst player still paid their $60 for the game. They deserve as much consideration and respect as anyone else. They want to play the game, so we should let them play!

Also, we can push back with any other data we have showing how skilled the player is: how many games in the series they've played, total hours played in the past month, significant achievements, etc. This can be convincing to designers, although ultimately it really isn't the point. Every player deserves to be able to progress.

You can also phrase your response as a question: "OK, so what percentage of players should quit here?" Any designer with a soul will respond "none."

"IT WON'T HAPPEN THAT OFTEN."

Pushing back against frequency is also quite common. Their argument is that the experience they've built works well almost all the time, and that fixing that weird edge case would take resources away from more important things.

Our counterargument: Why should this ever happen? If there were an intermittent technical bug that made players this unhappy, we'd make it a priority. There is no practical difference between a bug that makes player unable to progress and a poor user experience that makes a player turn off the game. The result is the same.

"IT WASN'T THAT BAD."

Another approach designers will take is to push back on the severity of the issue. Sure, that player was stuck for a bit, but they didn't die and they eventually figured it out. And it's true, not every issue is a UX apocalypse. Some problems are smaller than others. But at the same time, a researcher can't let issues just be ignored.

Our counterargument: Here's a video of the participant's expression. Here are their comments about the problem afterwards. Look those players in the eye and tell them you're not going to fix it. If the designer can do that with a clear conscience, so be it.

"BUT THAT'S MY VISION!"

Finally, the most frustrating response is when designers answer that what's happening is intentional. The player is supposed to struggle at this moment in the game, they're supposed to feel lost or hopeless or whatever. That's part of the larger emotional arc that the game is intended to build.

Our response: Is this little piece of the vision worth the potential cost to the rest of the vision? If the player quits now, they won't get a chance to see the big finale. All those other designers and artists put so much effort into all the subsequent levels of the game, and these players will never see any of that because this moment just had to be so damn punishing. We're not here to create one perfect moment, we're creating a much longer experience, and we need this part to serve the whole.

The end goal of a games researcher is to produce the best overall player experience. We have to fight for every issue, but in a way that doesn't poison the dialog for future issues. Whatever tactics or arguments we use to win this time need to be effective without leaving our partners feeling permanently hostile towards us. There's no point in winning today if we lose all subsequent arguments, but at the same time, our players deserve an advocate who fights hard for their needs.

Bringing the users' pain to the table is how we thread that needle. It's not us that's arguing, it's not us saying the game is bad, we're just the messengers. The designer can't get mad at us because we're just presenting the user's pain. We're not even really arguing with them; we're on the same side. We're not the prosecution, we're their defense attorney explaining the case against them so they can save themselves.

Of course, that's slightly disingenuous because as the owners of the study, we're responsible for collecting and curating the message as well. But as long as the message is a true picture of the user experience conveyed in good faith, a researcher's conscience is clear. And when the results are framed as the opinions of the players, not the researchers, the relationship between the researcher and the designer is preserved.

Designers should walk out of a usability session feeling like they've been beaten with hammers. Watching users fail at their content should be the hardest thing they do all week. Anything less potent will be washed away in the pressures of production schedules and competing priorities. They said they wanted to ship a good game, so you're helping them live up to their own ideals.

It is the researcher's job to craft studies that collect and focus user pain into a weapon. It's uncomfortable for everyone involved: the participants in the study, the researcher, the designer receiving the results.

But sparing everyone's feelings during development doesn't fix the problems. To find the issues and guarantee their resolution, we have to bring the pain.

CHAPTER 17
WHOSE IDEA WAS THIS STUDY ANYWAY?

Research studies are the natural byproduct of a good relationship between a researcher and their team. Some of the most common questions I get from new development partners are: "Where do the research topics come from? Do you pitch them or does the design team make requests?"

One correct answer is "both." There are times when designers ask for specific tests to be done and times when the research team will make pitches. An equally correct answer is "neither." The best ideas are organic outgrowths of the ongoing conversation between a researcher and the team they're supporting. That conversation should never stop; there should always be a steady stream of communication going both ways. Ideally, it should be hard to tell precisely where the idea for a study came from, because it should represent the combined perspective of everyone involved.

That being said, there are a few general categories of when design should and shouldn't ask for help, as well as a few clear situations when researchers should pitch their own ideas.

WHEN THE DESIGN TEAM SHOULD ASK FOR SOMETHING

Designers should always feel comfortable asking their researcher for data. That's what the researcher is there for, after all. The worst thing the researcher's going to say in response is "I don't know and I'm not sure when I'll have time to find out." Best case, the researcher already has the answer on hand. And if they don't, well, running studies is what they're here for.

In particular, designers should ask for studies when they feel they are taking a risk. Risks are good; we want our designers being creative and dramatic and inventing new things. But we don't want our players suffering because the new thing didn't work out. We want to put the new idea in front of players as soon as possible so we can validate it and then polish it into its best possible version.

This requires an admission of vulnerability on the part of the design team and a certain delicacy on the part of the researcher. The attitude of the researcher needs to be "I'm here to illuminate the proposed risk so the design team can make good decisions" not "is this a good idea?" As long as the design is within the bounds of ethics and good taste, it's not the researcher's job to approve the risk. We want designers to come to us with their craziest and most fragile ideas early. In fact, the crazier the idea, the earlier research should be involved. Designers won't do that if they think their precious creation will be judged unfairly.

A small caveat to the "always" rule is that designers should always ask for help with a topic, but they shouldn't necessarily ask for a specific test. Just as researchers sometimes make suggestions that miss important design nuances, designers sometimes request a style of test that won't actually answer the question at hand. Part of the researcher's job is negotiating with their team to settle on a method that is both appropriate and convincing to all stakeholders, which leads us to our next topic.

BAD REQUESTS

One special case of design team requests are situations where the request comes from an individual or faction intending to use the results as a cudgel against other members of the team. For example, a designer who has tried and failed to convince the rest of their team to change the level design might reach out to the research team for evidence to support their argument.

The right answer from the researcher to this request is not "no." We want the request, because it gives us a chance to serve the team by laying the contentious issue to rest. But the right answer isn't exactly "yes," either. It's more like "yes, but let's check with the other stakeholders." This is not intended to neutralize the request, but a way to guarantee the data has impact.

We want the results of the study to be persuasive to the whole team, not just the person who initially made the request. Even if the data does legitimately support their position, the point of the data isn't to convince the requester. After all, they already agree with it. The point of the data is to convince their skeptical colleagues, and the best way to do that is to engage with those colleagues ahead of time.

By engaging both sides of the argument and coming to an agreement about what data both sides would find convincing, you're going to create a cleaner study from the beginning and save yourself a lot of follow-up work.

This also highlights how essential it is that a researcher be in touch with their team's culture and discussions. Any request from the team might be a controversial topic, and research on such topics is only productive if we get the entire team involved early. Really, about half of all research requests have a trap buried in there somewhere. After all, if the entire design team agreed that a certain change needed to be made, they wouldn't be asking you, would they? They'd just do it! People ask for studies when they think other people need convincing, but for those studies to work then those other people need to be involved in the research process.

IDEAS FROM ABOVE

One special case of study pitches are those that come from management rather than from our peers on the design team. Like any other partner, studio management have real concerns and the research team can help validate or eliminate those concerns. Some examples of these kinds of questions are "is the game improving over time or are we just treading water?" or "is this feature/mode/mission worth finishing?" Keeping the game's production on track and making sure we hit the quality bar are legitimate worries and helping management with their concerns can be a great way to spread the gospel of user research and assure ourselves of top-down support in the studio.

However, there's a very real danger here of breaking the bond of trust with the design team. If designers begin to think of the research team as auditors, they're not going to be as open as they need to be to get the maximum benefit from user testing. The researcher must be a safe partner, someone who has demonstrated that they have the best interests of the thing you're making at heart. The concerns of management are different enough from those of the developers that it can come to feel like the researcher is being pulled between two masters.

The solution is to bring the design team into the loop, making sure they're fully bought into the work even if the idea didn't come from them. Framing the issue in terms of "what does this content need to succeed?" can be very powerful. You're not testing whether what they're making is bad; you're helping them ask management for the right amount of help.

If you ultimately can't convince the team that the test is in everyone's best interest, then the test is a dead issue. If it's run anyway, you'll be crippling the trust that's so vital to having research impact. If they think you are management's pet executioner, they will find excuses to put off testing until it's too late to help or hurt them.

WHEN THE RESEARCH TEAM SHOULD PITCH

Our partners need to believe that we as researchers are giving them true, neutral information. Pitching our own research ideas treads dangerously close to compromising that neutrality. After all, if you thought things were fine you wouldn't suggest wasting time checking them.

That said, here are a few of the situations where it's necessary for a researcher to speak up and propose a study:

When there is new information that is not being taken into account. Researchers often have access to information that designers don't, such as comments from previous studies or situations they've read about online. There's nothing wrong with bringing up that information for consideration by the team.

When the design breaks with common practice. There are standard UX best practices, and designers sometimes violate them in the hopes of producing a better experience. For example, players shouldn't be required to remember things from one screen to another, such as when comparing two pieces of equipment. Sometimes these rules are broken on purpose, sometimes by accident. In either case, it's a researcher's duty to make sure players are OK with it.

When the design matches old designs that were broken. Just as there are well known successful design patterns, there are also patterns that often cause problems. An example of this might be having a sharp difficulty spike in the middle of a mission, or an objective that requires players to backtrack through content they've already cleared.

When there are unacknowledged risks being taken. For example, games sometimes cut one piece of content that may or may not have other impacts. That's a risk to the player experience, and a simple user test where players skip over that content can confirm whether the risk is worth it.

A good pitch from a researcher often starts with gathering more information from the design team. It might sound something like this: "Hey folks, I'm concerned about X for reasons Y and Z. How do you feel about X?" As I mentioned earlier, good studies grow out of conversations between researchers and designers, so the ideal pitch from a researcher is essentially just a specialized conversation starter.

BAD PITCHES

The one case where researchers should NOT pitch studies is when they just personally disagree with the design choices. Every researcher is tempted by this at least occasionally. After all, ideas for research projects come from highly subjective sources all the time: a forum post, a playtest comment, a designer's intuition. If everyone else in the process gets to be subjective, why not the researcher themselves?

But our suggestions cannot be based on anything but hard data. The risk isn't about creating one biased study. The danger is that the team will begin to perceive the researcher as just another opinion. The goal of user research is to create the greatest possible net improvement to the game and allowing our studies to become tainted with personal bias damages not just the studies in question but all future work with the team.

WHEN TO SAY NO

Saying no to a study request is excruciating for researchers. Running studies is what we do; we wouldn't be in this job if we didn't like doing it. Also, it actually takes a fair amount of work to build up the relationship with a developer to the point where they're asking for studies. Turning down the opportunity can feel like a tremendous waste, but sometimes it's necessary.

Most reasons to turn down a study fall into the general category of the study not having impact. For example, sometimes teams will ask for something to be tested too late, after the point where changes are no longer possible. Or a study might be requested by one party, but the rest of the team doesn't agree or believe in it. If the study is not going to lead to meaningful change in the game, it shouldn't be run.

Another strong reason to say no is when you won't believe the results of your own study. Not all topics are equally testable and it is the researcher's job to understand their own limitations and say "no" when a study goes beyond the bounds. A good example of this would be studies that would require players to predict their own behavior in a hypothetical future situation. We know from plenty of behavioral economics studies that people are not good at that sort of prediction, and it's much easier to nip the idea before the study happens than to try to prevent the design team from drawing bad conclusions afterwards.

IT JUST HAPPENED

This might seem counterintuitive, but the best answer to the question "who proposed this study?" is always "I don't remember. We were talking about the game and it just happened." Good studies grow out of good relationships between research and design. When the team is comfortable with their support and has participated in the process before, they'll be tossing out requests and ideas that sound like they're coming from researchers. When a researcher has been invited to enough design meetings and has internalized the team's priorities and needs, they'll find themselves proposing ideas before the team can ask for them.

CHAPTER 18
TURNING THE FLYWHEEL

When working with a new team, I often find it useful to volunteer to do surveys or other research studies on practical topics around the office. It's a cheap and effective way to introduce myself to people and to promote the idea that research is both interesting and approachable. A lot of people assume user research is a complicated, expensive process with long lead times, so they're reluctant to approach us with requests or ideas. Tossing out a quick survey on some topic that's interesting to the average employee establishes that research is agile and relevant and opens a lot of doors for more impactful future projects.

Which is all by way of explaining why I once spent an entire day doing a survey about French fries. It was my first month at a new company and there had been a debate on an internal company chat about which chains had the best fries. I offered to settle the debate by running a quick survey and creating a simple dashboard of the results. Sure, it was silly, but it made every single coworker who participated aware that I existed, that I had the tools for doing research, and that I was an approachable person who didn't take myself too seriously. I can trace several different real game projects to this one survey on French fries, just because it made people more willing to reach out to me.

This study was completely useless by every metric but the most important one: it improved the environment for user research at the company. The survey itself was a quick bit of throwaway work, but it also made the next study happen sooner and easier than it would have if I'd stuck to serious research. In other words, the French fry survey turned the flywheel.

In his book *Good to Great*, James Colins describes the concept of "turning the flywheel," creating a virtuous cycle of success. In this paradigm, a business should be organized around a cycle of actions where each step has a positive impact on the next step. If that cycle is a closed loop, this creates a self-perpetuating rising tide of improvements.

For games user research, the flywheel looks like this:

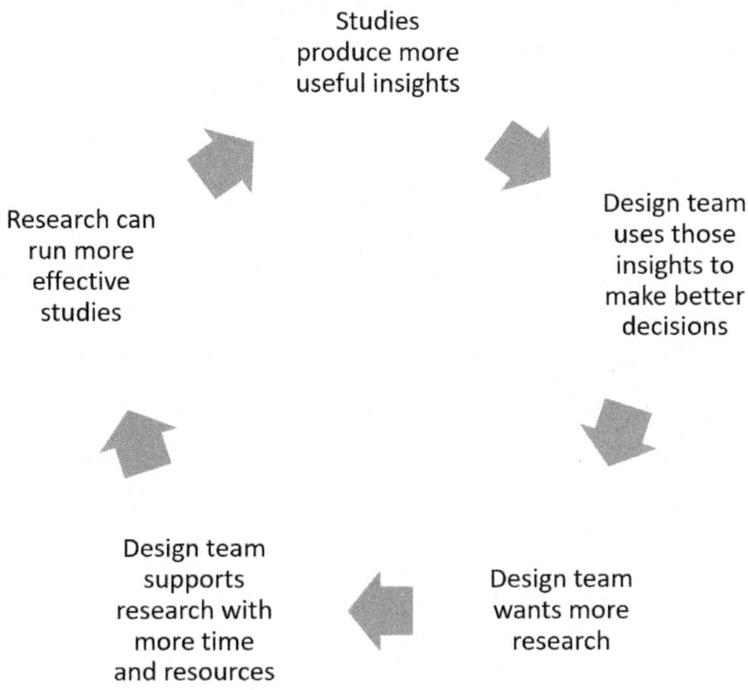

The user research flywheel

Under this model, good individual studies are not sufficient. No matter how accurate the results, any single study will fail if the resulting momentum doesn't make it all the way around the loop. It's not enough to just deliver insights, the insights must result in tangible value to the design team. Without seeing that value, they won't invest in future research and that additional investment is what enables research to really get off the ground.

Looked at this way, once the flywheel starts turning and gathering momentum, the effect becomes self-sustaining. It doesn't matter how simple or grudging the first studies on a new game are if they nudge the flywheel into motion. Once it's turning, things will naturally get better. Every study hits a little harder than the last as trust and investment increase.

From this perspective, a good study is one that creates more studies through the intervening steps of providing value to the team and generating buy-in. Certainly, we want the study to have impact on its own, but it also needs to make the next study happen sooner, be bigger, have more impact. We're not here to win once and walk away; each study is a small part of a much larger effort: building an organization that uses data to ship the best games possible.

What follows are some steps a researcher can take to start that flywheel and keep it turning.

STARTING EARLY

A good example of this progression is the change in when studies happen during development. It's very common for a studio that has never dealt with research before to think of it as a grade on their work, so they naturally put off research until as late in the process as possible to get the highest grade. But once they've done it on one game, it's less scary and therefore they're willing to let testing happen a little earlier. On *Halo 2*, we were only allowed to really start testing about 6 months before the game shipped. For *Halo 3*, we were allowed to start farther out, 18 months. A few games later, by the time Bungie made *Destiny 1*, we were testing the game 4 years before it shipped. Sure, it's frustrating to know that there were opportunities lost on the earlier games because we weren't allowed to do our jobs as early as we wanted, but things have to start somewhere. We get better at doing our jobs, and our partners get better at integrating us into their projects.

STARTING SMALL

User research is primarily about inserting the user perspective into the design process, which inevitably involves overruling the designer's intuition at least part of the time. That experience isn't always pleasant for the designer, and they often push back on the inclusion of research, especially early on in development.

Fortunately, in a model of slowly growing momentum we don't need to go big at the start. Anything that gets the wheel turning is fine, and in fact there's a lot to be said for making the initial steps as small and harmless as possible. We just need to get things rolling, to start building trust and investment safely. The amount of impact a researcher has is proportional to the trust available, so there's no point to swinging for the fences. Just create momentum, and eventually small victories will create the environment for larger victories.

These early projects don't even need to be about the game. There are all sorts of situations where research expertise is useful, such as the French fry example above. I've run internal elections, employee morale surveys, and many other things that aren't actually about games. But every research-like project builds relationship and awareness, which contributes to the necessary momentum and lays the groundwork for real game impact. At one company, I ran a New Year's resolution project, designed to help people who'd decided to get healthier stick to their exercise resolutions. It wasn't strictly what I was being paid to do, but it was beneficial to the studio and let me introduce ideas about data tracking and metrics to a broad cross-section of my coworkers.

LOW EFFORT = LOW RISK

It's also worth noting that early projects with new teams fail a lot. There can be plenty of reasons for this, including not having the necessary buy-in for the study to have impact, or simply running the wrong test. Every game is different, and what might be the right thing to test on one game might be completely wrong on another. There's always a discovery period where the researcher throws things at the wall to see what sticks. In keeping with this model, it's important to make those early trials fast and cheap, making it easy and painless to fail until an approach is discovered that starts the flywheel turning.

This is closely related to the "lean" model of software development, where the goal is to develop the simplest possible thing (a "minimum viable product") that people will pay for. Once you have that, you can iterate to improve it. But far too many companies spend years building things before establishing contact with their customers, and a lot of them are in for a shock when their untested product hits the market. Rather than try to present a development partner with a pre-built research package with all the bells and whistles, contact can be made humbly, and the value of research established before any massive investment is required.

(You'll notice this is the same argument for why user research needs to exist at all. We get the dev team in contact with their customers early to understand their needs, but the best way to make that happen is to get in touch with *our* customers on the dev team and understanding the dev team's needs. It's listening to the user all the way down.)

HARD LESSONS

One humbling takeaway from the flywheel model of research is how little of the process is in the researcher's hands. We can directly control the quality of our research, but every other step is in the hands of the development team. The only place where our technical research skills matter is in the actual study itself. Everything else is about soft skills and diplomacy, working with the design team to turn the data into decisions and those decisions into trust. That's why my hiring is always focused more on soft skills than technical know-how. It's easier to train a new hire in a specific query language or a particular survey tool than it is to teach persuasion and people skills. The job is about shepherding the results around the circle much more than it is about the creation of the initial results themselves.

Another frustrating takeaway is that there is no definition of a perfect study in isolation. Just as a shark that's supremely adapted to the ocean would be helpless on land, a research study that is ideally suited to one team and studio might be a complete failure at another in another place and time. An ideal study meets the team where they are. We can't just learn to do a perfect playtest and repeat it forever, because "perfect" is a moving target. Similarly, we can't take a case study from another company and apply it directly to our work. A good study is bespoke, tailored to the client by someone who understands both research and the organization they're trying to help.

Finally, it's important to be careful that these early projects don't create limits on the rest of the relationship. It might make sense to run something fast and simple because it's early days and there's no point in investing more, but it sets an expectation that all studies are that simple, or that simple studies are all that's possible. These early studies need to be framed as trials, explorations, or even throwaways. This helps lower the bar for those early studies at the same time, making them seem less rigid and threatening. An "experiment" is much less scary than "this is how you'll be graded now and forever."

One of the most painful lessons for newcomers to the games user research field is that just running good research studies isn't enough. A researcher obviously should be running good studies, but the definition of "good" is more slippery and elusive than it might appear at first glance. To my mind, a good study is one that's accurate and useful, but also needs to help foster an environment where the next study is set up for even more success.

Similarly, research is never an end in itself; it only has value when it makes the game better. We will always have to depend on the rest of the team and the process for validation. The ideal study is one that is just slightly better than the team deserves, that outperforms expectations by just enough to raise trust and investment, causing the flywheel to speed up with the least wasted effort. While it's tempting to just skip to the endgame, going straight to "real" studies, those studies can't survive unless the groundwork has already been laid. It would be like building a high-performance car in the eighteenth century, without having a supporting ecosystem of good roads, gas stations, etc. We want the most impact currently possible with a minimum of wastage.

The limiting factor of research impact is always the relationship with the rest of the development team. Therefore, the best research is that which moves the relationship forward. The results of the research must always be true, of course, but there are lots of true things we could discover at any given point in time. The real skills of the researcher are to learn the right true thing at the right time, and to foster a continually improving environment so those truths can have the maximum impact.

Note that this is not a decision that the researcher has to make in isolation. Our partners are grown-ups (the anime figurines on their desks notwithstanding) and should have a say in what research we do.

But it's ultimately the researcher's responsibility to take the team's requests and filter it through their own experience and judgment.

A research team with a working flywheel will inevitably succeed. Once the virtuous cycle is established, the research team's value naturally grows with every study. It can feel painfully slow at the start, but as momentum builds victory for both the team and the game becomes certain.

CHAPTER 19
MAKING RECOMMENDATIONS

After finding a problem, the natural next step is to suggest a solution. This is where many games user researchers undercut all the good work they've just done. The last thing we want to do is act like every other fan and make amateur design suggestions that destroy our credibility. However, if we don't make recommendations, we end up looking like data-driven complainers and designers will start avoiding us in the hallway. We need to navigate between the two extremes by making good suggestions that drive the design process forward without pretending to be junior designers ourselves.

Remember, **the essential goal of recommendations is to improve the game**. It is never ever to make our own ideas happen. The true definition of "recommendation" for a games researcher is not "a specific suggestion for a change the design team should make to fix the issue." Rather, it is "a thing the researcher says after stating the facts of issue which leads to the design team constructively debating solutions among themselves." The true barrier to making a better game is not disagreement, it's apathy. The point of a good recommendation is to create momentum, to encourage the team to engage with the problem.

Here are a few concrete tips for creating suggestions that actually get done:

First, **make sure the team wants recommendations**. Not all teams do, and their experiences with other researchers in the past may have left them with well justified scars. Especially in the early part of the relationship with a new team, it can be better to establish research as a safe but dull appliance that churns out data. Once they believe the data and you know these people better, you can be more aggressive in pushing the team towards a solution. When in doubt, ask them what they want from you. Their answer doesn't have to constrain you forever, but it can be a good starting place.

Next, **try asking questions rather than making suggestions**. Start with "given these results, do you think the boss fight needs to be made easier?" or even "why do you think so many participants had trouble with that room?" The key here is that you're still deferring to them as the design owner, making it clear they're the expert and in control of what happens to their game. This also puts you in a non-adversarial relationship with the designer. You're not telling them what to do, just asking the right questions. It's very rare for designers to say they're just going to leave the problem as is. However, "will not fix" is as valid a response to design bugs as it is to technical bugs.

One version of asking questions is simply to **leave a space for "next steps"** or "proposed fix" after each issue in your reports and ask them to help you fill it out. It's not you that's demanding that they do something, you're just filling in the form. Again, this leaves the designer in control of their content, and you're their helpful assistant making sure their intent is properly logged. This kind of "next steps" tracking is useful in any case, even when you do full recommendations as well, because the chosen course of action is generally not the precise suggestion the researcher made.

Similarly, **use solutions discussed by the design team during the study**. During a study, designers will often mention potential solutions to you and to each other, and those offhand comments are a gold mine of potential recommendations. You're not here to be creative or original; you're trying to make sure that the issue gets fixed. The designers you're working with know their own constraints and capabilities better than you do, and even their most offhand idea is probably better than anything you'll come up with. Give them credit, certainly, but always use their own words as a starting place if you can. Best of all, this doesn't even come across as a suggestion. It's just you being a good secretary: "What about the idea you mentioned about moving the door to the other wall?"

Remember: **Suggestions should never be phrased as demands or requirements.** "Make the boss easier" comes across as a challenge to the designer's authority. By telling them how the game should have been designed, you're claiming to be a better designer than they are. Instead, come at it from a place of "*consider*", "*think about,*" "*evaluate,*" or even "*explore.*" The designer can take those suggestions without feeling like they're taking dictation. You asked them to consider it, they did, and maybe they'll implement it and maybe they won't. The designer's mental immune system is more likely to kill a suggestion than the suggestion's actual content. By taking a soft approach, you're making sure that you don't set off their defenses and ensuring that they at least listen.

Next, **a good suggestion always acknowledges the constraints of the development team.** Just as a leader should never give an order that won't be obeyed, a researcher should never make a recommendation that is impossible to implement. Making technically or logistically impossible suggestions burns your credibility, so you've not only failed to fix this problem, you've made fixing the next one harder. By paying attention in meetings with the development team, you can learn where they are in the schedule and what kinds of tasks can still be done right now. For example, the layout of a map is often locked down before the rest of a level design. Asking for the map layout to be fundamentally changed late in the development cycle is just going to flag you as a dilettante. But you can probably get a tooltip or the placement of an enemy changed right up until the end. Know what your team can do, and what they were already planning to do. Whenever possible, ask for changes that can be made as part of the natural flow of work rather than a separate task. For example, if you know that there is an upcoming weapon balance pass on the dev schedule, fold your recommendation into the pass. The designer will already have the appropriate file open and they're already in the mindset to make that type of change, so your request becomes a matter of seconds rather than a separate task.

One general rule of thumb is that **changes to numbers are easier to accomplish** than anything else. Art, music, recorded dialogue, character models… all of these are expensive and difficult to change. But making a gun do two points less damage or the enemy start at slightly different coordinates are cheap options. When in doubt, ask for tuning rather than rebuilding. Again, this shows that you're an insider, a professional, one of them. All their defenses are tuned to keep outsiders out.

Similarly, **removing things from the game is always easier** than adding or changing them. Take one of the enemies out of a battle to make it easier, hide an unnecessary button, remove a distracting visual effect, all of these take much less work to change. They're also changes that are simple to reverse if they don't work out. Make it easy for your team to say yes.

Having spent several pages arguing for parsimony, don't be surprised if **the size of the suggested changes has no relationship to the difficulty of implementation**. Sometimes small changes are harder than large changes. For example, I once asked for the designers to remove an enemy or two from an encounter, and it turned out that was a monumental task in that game because the enemies were being spawned by a global algorithm. Changing it in that instance would have meant either altering a feature that affected the entire game or breaking that encounter off into a special case, something that comes with its own hidden costs. Every game has its own quirks, and what's easy to change in one game might be impossible in another and vice versa. An informal conversation where ideas are spit-balled freely can sometimes lead to surprising results.

Another example of this was the *Knights of the Frozen Throne* expansion for the *Hearthstone* card game. When playtesting showed that some of the early fights in the story mode were too hard and some of the later fights were too easy, my research team made the standard, conservative recommendation to nerf the early ones and buff the later ones. Instead, what the designers did was *sort* the fights, moving the easy fights earlier in the sequence and the harder ones towards the end. Because *Hearthstone* adventures were a sequence of boss fights with minimal connective tissue, the designers had a unique solution available to them that isn't available in most games. They used what was special about their game to fix the problem quickly and easily, in a way that would never have occurred to me as an outsider.

Personally, I've always felt the best response a designer can give me to one of my suggestions is "no, but...", as in "no, we can't do X but we could do Y." Even the worst idea from a designer is more likely to get implemented than the best idea from a non-designer. Even once the idea is proposed and agreed to, the actual implementation of the idea isn't a sure thing. Our hypothetical solution must survive in an ecosystem of other tasks all fighting for their spot on the team's busy development schedule, and its chances of surviving that Darwinian process are much higher if the implementer feels personal ownership of the fix.

It's also worth pointing out that the researcher on a game will be making a lot of suggestions over the course of months and even years. Our job is to have the largest possible overall impact, even if that means letting a particular suggestion go. It is extremely rare for an individual suggestion to be worth burning bridges with the team. Every suggestion needs to be made in a way that doesn't damage all the other suggestions that come after it.

A researcher's job is never to tell a designer how to design their game. It's to say and do what it takes to help them be better designers. A good recommendation gets their thinking started, gets them engaged and motivated. It's not the ultimate solution, it's just a step on the road to the real answer.

CHAPTER 20
OPTIMIZING FOR COMMUNICATION

During the development of *Halo Wars,* I traveled to the Ensemble offices to convince them of the value my research team could contribute to the game. After I arrived, I was left in a conference room while my escort went off to round up the other attendees for the meeting. I booted up my laptop and looked around, noticing that the walls of the conference room displayed several pieces of concept art for the new game. I quickly opened my presentation and changed all the names in my examples to match the labels on the pictures on the walls. When the team showed up for the meeting, my pitch went over like a dream, skipping right past the usual debate about the basic value of the data to a much more interesting discussion of what was the right data and what decisions they needed to make. The team was also very concerned that the names had somehow leaked to the public!

The hard part of games user research is rarely the technical challenge of executing a research study. Instead, it's getting the development team to participate with the study and then act on the results. In most game studios, researchers don't have the authority to make designers listen to them and really, no one who cares about the end product would want researchers to be in charge. While there are some corners of the industry that are truly "data-driven" and practice design by focus group and A/B test, they produce horrific game-shaped objects rather than actual games.

So, researchers exist in the role of advisers and influencers. Our results must be not just true, but *convincing*. This task is made more complicated by the fact that everyone else is also trying to convince the decision makers. Designers' ideological immune systems don't always distinguish between good, data-based ideas and someone else's personal crusade to nerf snipers. There's a high bar for our data to overcome before we can impact the game.

A research study has no value until the results are conveyed to the development team, and dev teams often avoid data like tight-lipped children resisting bitter medicine. I've often found myself wishing the observation room of my usability lab came equipped with chairs with straps, so I could force my designers to sit and watch what real players go through in their games. In fairness, they do genuinely have competing priorities, and many designers have suffered at the hands of those who believe data should demand instead of advise.

From one point of view, there is an ideal world where the decision makers don't have to see the results themselves. Their time is valuable and attending a study can be a large commitment. Researchers tell ourselves that if we were good enough, the designers would just take our word for the results and make changes in the game accordingly. But realistically, we need to produce an artifact (a report, a presentation, an email, a bug) that is not just accurate, but intentionally tailored for ease of absorption by the design culture.

As in the *Halo Wars* example above, one vital tool for making sure research has maximum impact is to **use the same language as the design team**. Learn the terms the designers and engineers use and phrase your results using those terms. This gives you instant credibility. Using the language of the design team makes your work more comprehensible, but it also marks you as part of the in-crowd. As I said earlier, designers are buried in suggestions from outsiders. The more your suggestions match how the team talks to each other, the more they'll listen.

Similarly, **use their communications channels.** Different teams have different preferred ways of talking to each other. Some teams only really communicate by email, some have key meetings where decisions are made, some live out of their bug database. It's the researcher's job to meet the team wherever they are, using whatever tools they use. Again, all design teams have powerful immune systems to protect themselves from outsiders, but by slipping results and suggestions into the channels they're already listening to, a researcher can bypass several lines of defense.

One special case of this principle is **finding an advocate on the development team** to act or speak for the research. By definition, those on the team are already integrated into the usual communications of the team, so if they send out a meeting request or a playtest report, the rest of the team is a lot more likely to open the email and internalize the results. Development teams are often insular and tribal, so the duty of a researcher is to either pass as part of the tribe they're trying to influence or find someone within the tribe to serve as an advocate.

Finally, **optimizing for communication starts with hiring.** When recruiting researchers, the ability to convey results in a way that's both accurate and persuasive is the single most important hiring criteria. This is not to say that running a good study should be taken for granted and we should just hire salesmen. But it is easier to teach someone with social skills to do good research than it is to teach someone with strong research skills to be a social influencer. The technical details of how to run a study aren't anywhere near as complicated as the personalities and social structures that determine whether a study has impact.

PART FOUR
CASE STUDIES

CHAPTER 21
THE TIME I TRIED TO RUIN HALO 2

THE GAME

When *Halo 2* was released in 2004, it instantly became the most popular multiplayer game on Xbox Live, and it held that position against all challengers for almost two years. A decent argument can be made that the primary reason Xbox Live survived its infancy was the massive popularity of this single title. During the game's six-year lifetime, more than 6.6 million players played over 499 million hours of *Halo 2* online multiplayer. The development team at Bungie took a bold risk in building a new type of online experience and it was a massive success and made literally millions of people happy.[1]

Which is why I'm glad I didn't succeed in killing it in the lab.

THE PROPHETS

During development, *Halo 2* was codenamed "Prophets" after the new race of aliens being added to the Halo universe in the sequel to the groundbreaking *Halo: Combat Evolved*. At the time, most researchers at

Microsoft supported three to five titles each, but because this was a major tent pole title for the original Xbox, there were two user experience researchers assigned to help with the game full time, myself and Randy Pagulayan. Both of us were trained scientists with PhD's in experimental psychology and early members of Microsoft's groundbreaking Games User Research team. Our job was to use qualitative and quantitative techniques like usability studies, playtests, and surveys to give the design team insights into how the game would be received after it was released.

This is a story about a time when I failed to be a good prophet, where my attempts to project research data into the future led to a conflict between the research team at Microsoft and the design team at Bungie. Usually, public discussions about games user research focus on the times we were right, the times when data fixed game design. This story is one of the other times, when two otherwise competent researchers drew the wrong conclusions about an innovative piece of game design, made bad recommendations, and how the game succeeded despite our "help."

THE INNOVATION

Prior to *Halo 2*, most online games didn't have matchmaking. Instead, the default solution to finding other people to play with online was to use lobby systems. Players would select a lobby (a virtual waiting room) from a list, using the short descriptions written by the lobbies' creators to decide which one was right for them. If the lobby turned out to be occupied by jerks or much better players, you could back out and choose a new lobby to suit your tastes.

The great advantage of these lobby systems was control. The lobby creator had the ability to set up a highly curated experience, allowing just the maps, game modes, and settings that they liked, kicking out players who didn't play their way. It was routine to see lobbies that proudly announced "no snipers" or "<specific map name> free-for-all only".

In contrast, the proposed *Halo 2* system took almost all choices away, replacing them with a system where players only got to choose the general type of match (e.g., Free for all, Big Team Battle, etc.) and then Bungie would choose the map, gametype, and the opponents.

Here's how GameSpy described the *Halo 2* system in an article published before the game was released:

> "...In an interesting twist, the gametypes, maps, vehicles, and just about everything else are set by Bungie.
>
> While this might sound weird at first, it's a good idea for a number of reasons. By guaranteeing that everyone is optimized for the same type of game, Bungie can ensure that all of the games will run smoothly. They can also be positive that all the rankings will be consistent, since nearly everyone will be playing on the same maps with roughly the same number of players. At any time, they can just push some updates to Xbox Live, and everyone will be playing new games. The ranking system is set up by match type, so you might be #25 in the Assault mode, but only #78 in Slayer..."

This description sounds incredibly mundane and obvious now, but that's because this system succeeded so well that it became the new standard for all multiplayer games going forward. *Halo 2* won so completely that it's hard to imagine how online play worked before.

Again, I'm really glad I wasn't able to kill it.

THE RESEARCH

Our task as researchers was to make sure players would understand the new paradigm. Since it was so different from what our players were used to and from what had been done in the first *Halo* game, we wanted to put the new design in front of real players as early as possible, starting with paper prototypes and written descriptions. Players were shown descriptions and wireframe interfaces for several different options of how they could play multiplayer games, including the new matchmaking system and private games, but not including traditional user-created lobbies.

The overwhelming reaction we got from our participants was "we understand but we hate it." Almost unanimously, the players we talked to told us they wanted the level of personal control a lobby system gave them and didn't think the benefits of the new matchmaking system were worth what they were giving up. It's hard to imagine now, but the "push one button and trust us" approach came across as creepy and controlling to players who were used to choosing for themselves.

Seeing ourselves as righteous champions of the users, Randy and I went to Bungie and told them that players hated the new design and that we should consider other ways of doing matchmaking. The designers stuck to their guns, insisting that their vision of the future was better than the status quo, and history has proven them absolutely right. Players loved the new system, and it became the gold standard for online gameplay. The *Halo 2* matchmaking study remains the single biggest "miss" of my career. (So far, anyway.)

THE MISTAKES

What happened? How did our study produce results so at odds with what actually happened after release? The answer is two intertwined mistakes, one made by the participants and one made by the researchers.

The participants' mistake was engaging in "affective forecasting"—guessing how they'd feel in a hypothetical situation. There's an amazing amount of literature about how bad humans are at estimating how hypothetical situations will affect them emotionally. Even big life changing events such as becoming paraplegic or winning the lottery are difficult to judge in the abstract.

If you'd asked the research team at the time, we would have responded that of course humans are bad at affective forecasting, but that wasn't really what we were doing. Our study originally began as "will players understand this system?"—a legitimate research question that we were able to answer with a solid "yes." But when participants also expressed opinions about the system, we treated those opinions as truth rather than as guesses.

The crux of the problem was that our participants had never experienced an online shooter with real matchmaking. Again, this seems ridiculous now, because matchmaking is now a standard feature in every online multiplayer game. But at the time, most of our participants had only played multiplayer on their local network or, at most, on a dorm network. Less than 16% of Americans had broadband when we ran this study in 2003. We were effectively asking our participants to make a judgment between a known experience (current lobbies) and an unknown experience (fair and accurate online matchmaking in a large online population). For the current system, they understood both the costs and benefits. For the proposed system of matchmaking, they could only really understand what they were giving up. This made the proposed system seem like a much worse change to them than it actually was.

So when our participants told us that they would not enjoy the system, we as researchers then made our own mistake and conveyed those comments as accurately representing how most players would feel about the system after they'd actually played it. And after some heated arguments and back and forth, Bungie chose to push on ahead with their novel matchmaking system over our objections, which turned out to be exactly the right call.

Of course, when the Bungie designers overruled the research team, they weren't pointing out our methodological flaws or making an argument against affective forecasting. They had a uniquely clear design vision which had been built on solid principles and then hotly debated within the studio, producing a battle-hardened belief on the part of key engineering and design leaders that this was the way to produce a great multiplayer experience. One of them privately told me afterwards that no possible set of results from this study would have convinced them to change course. When I present research findings to teams and get overruled like this, I almost always get to say "I told you so" in some highly professional way after the game ships. But on *Halo 2*, the other side of the argument turned out to be absolutely correct and the gaming world is better for it.

What we as researchers should have done is be more discriminating in how we presented the results. Our data was completely true when looked at from a specific angle: "Here's what some players will say when they hear about the system for the first time." From there, we could have worked with the team to test different ways of presenting the system to improve that first impression and increase the speed at which players realized the true value of the system. The data wasn't fundamentally bad, if only we hadn't taken it at face value.

THE LESSONS

I've thought quite a bit about this incident since, and here are a few of the lessons I took away. Hopefully, sharing this story will allow others to skip past these particular mistakes and make more interesting new mistakes of their own.

Lesson 1: Sometimes researchers should lose the argument.

UX researchers tend to get into the habit of thinking that we are discovering capital T Truth. This can lead to a lot of frustration when other parties in the development process don't accept our findings. Now, we're usually right, but false positives, false negatives, and outright mistakes are always possible.

Games user research is a vital voice in the development process even though we're no more perfect than anyone else involved. We're supposed to advocate passionately for our understanding of the player experience but we're not always meant to win. In fact, I'd argue that, just like for the players in our games, there is an ideal level of failure for researchers. If every study is equally successful, it just means that we aren't innovating enough or taking on challenging research topics. We need to take risks, and that means we have to lose sometimes.

Lesson 2: Being wrong isn't the end of the research relationship.

The *Halo 2* user research effort was an intense experience. Microsoft made a heavy bet on this one title, dedicating a level of research bandwidth that would have supported half a dozen games. Bungie, a studio that was notoriously selective about their partners, took a leap of faith in allowing us unprecedented access to their development process during one of the fiercest crunches in their history. There was enormous pressure on Randy and me to deliver value, to turn user feedback into design impact on a game that was important to so very many people. Faced with a clear message from our participants, terrified that the design was going to negatively affect the experiences of millions of players, we made the decision that this was a fight we needed to have. We were wrong and we lost.

This story happened in 2003, in the middle of the *Halo 2* development cycle, and we went on to do quite a number of other successful studies on the game. After it shipped, Randy and I dove into supporting the sequel, *Halo 3*, which became one of the most successful games user research efforts ever. The same two researchers, the same designers, the same franchise; this time, our work ended up on the cover of Wired magazine and was a major milestone in the adoption of user research in the games industry. In fact, this study and its failure directly contributed to those subsequent successes. One of the conclusions that Bungie leadership drew was that research needed to be more closely integrated with the design team to prevent this kind of thing from happening again, and that integration was key to our *Halo 3* effort. I even went on to be hired directly by Bungie to create and lead their own internal research team a few years later.

Researchers aren't perfect, but our partners don't actually need us to be perfect. They need us to honestly represent the player voice to the best of our ability, to push ourselves to innovate and take risks, and to admit and adapt when we're wrong.

Lesson 3: Research and design operate on the same playing field by different rules.

Players can only speak from their own experience, either in their past play or what's immediately in front of them in the lab. Since a researcher's job boils down to amplifying the player voice, we share the same limitation. Our prophecies are only as true as what the players are reacting to.

Designers don't share that limitation. They can come up with ideas that bear little or no relation to what's come before, which can make those ideas difficult to test early enough to do any good. There are ways to evaluate novel ideas, but as researchers we need to recognize that those ways are much riskier than our other tools and temper our conclusions accordingly.

Ironically, a good counterexample of presenting a novel experience in an understandable way was demonstrated by the Bungie team themselves during the development of *Halo 2*. The matchmaking system discussed here was only one part of a larger set of new multiplayer features introduced in *Halo 2*, and many of the other features encountered similar resistance. In order to convince skeptical Microsoft execs, the design team created a video simulating what playing with friends would be like in the final product. While this particular solution wouldn't have worked for matchmaking, it's an example of the extra level of effort and creativity it takes to convey novel experiences.

Lesson 4: Making methodological mistakes and facing their consequences is the best way to understand research design.

I certainly knew about the problems with affective forecasting before this study. But I still let myself be drawn in by the participants' strong opinions of the new system and presented their forecasts as facts. Having had that happen once and experienced the humiliating consequences, I've been a lot less prone to making that particular error ever since.

It's all well and good to memorize the principles of good research design, but you will never feel them in your bones until you violate those principles and experience the results firsthand. It doesn't matter if you broke the rules intentionally or if there were extenuating circumstances. Having to throw out days or weeks of hard work due to methodological problems leaves useful scars. Coloring outside the lines can be the best way to learn why the lines were needed in the first place.

But the other thing you discover is that sometimes… you get away with it. Some rules of good research turn out to have the force of natural law, while others are merely guidelines. Games user research is an applied field, done at breakneck speed with limited resources under messy conditions. Not every study is going to be a perfect jewel of experimental design. Stakeholders will push for changes to the study plan, participants will fail to show up, equipment will break, and the job of a researcher becomes about choosing the least damaging way to adjust to circumstance. Understanding which principles have flex to them and which are inviolable makes us better researchers, able to adapt and deliver the greatest value to our teams and our games.

AFTERWORD

Innovative design means taking risks, and in this case the risks taken by the Bungie design team paid off in spectacular fashion. The larger role of user research in the development process is about helping to offset those design risks, enabling our designers to try new things while detecting and fixing potential problems before they frustrate real players. But inside of our profession, we're also taking our own little risks, making judgment calls about study designs and which issues are worth fighting for. The choices we made in this case didn't pay off, but that doesn't change the fact that research risks are necessary. A good researcher will always have to use their experience and their gut to take just the right level of risks to be the best possible partners to our designers and produce the best game for our players.

(Special thanks to Randy Pagulayan for helping with this chapter and for being brave enough to share the public shame with me. And thanks to Chris Butcher, David Candland, Curtis Creamer, Max Hoberman, and Jason Jones for helping to refresh my memory about this story and for suggestions on the best way to tell it.)

CHAPTER 22
TALKING TO SUPERVILLAINS

Interviews are the purest form of user research: just sitting down and talking to players. They seem almost too simple to be a legitimate method of scientific inquiry, but their very minimalism ensures them a permanent place in our toolbox. Where interviews shine is as a tool of exploration. Because they are so simple and so quick, they're a great first pass at understanding what players think on any given topic.

Interviews are also infinitely flexible since they're not restrained by what's in the game (or even if there is a game at all). When you don't know what you're going to find, you have to have a human in the loop to interpret what the participants are saying. Interviews are fully interactive in a way other forms of research are not.

When you work in games, it's very common to deal with players in the abstract. We get in the habit of thinking of players in terms of categories ("hardcore", "casual", etc.) and can lose sight of the real people behind the labels. Interviews turn stereotypes back into individuals. Statistics are cool, but nothing can ever generate empathy on the part of the design team faster than looking into a player's eyes as they talk about the game.

This is true for researchers as well as for the rest of the dev team. We are here to advocate for our players, to preach the gospel of the user to our colleagues. It can be hard to maintain the right level of enthusiasm, to advocate fiercely day in and day out for years on end. Push-back from the rest of the team and lost arguments can wear anyone down. But one of the fastest ways I've found to re-spark that passion in myself is doing interviews, having the players talk to me directly, human to human.

This case study is about a set of group interviews (focus groups) we did with one of the least understood types of gamer, and how those interviews helped us grow a game in the right direction for them and for the rest of the players.

The term "gamer" has basically become synonymous with "angry nerd." Between real world toxicity of Gamergate, swatting, and the general miasma of hostility experienced in most online multiplayer spaces, gamers have a (mostly deserved) poor reputation.

Every multiplayer game design involves some work to address toxicity. We create systems to allow players to report misbehavior and systems for banning players who receive too many reports. We monitor chat channels to detect forbidden words and even sanction famous tournament players when they prove to be bad examples to the community.

What we don't do very often with toxic players is talk to them. We treat them as supervillains, inherently bad actors with irredeemably evil motives. They are to be identified and banned, or even isolated on special villain-only servers where they can only torment each other.

Don't get me wrong, I'm as opposed to toxic behavior as anyone, and I'm certainly not calling for pity or leniency for these players when they act out. But I do believe that we're failing both them and the rest of our players when we neglect to study their motives as thoroughly as we do the motives of other groups in our games. If we were doing our jobs correctly, the game would be built such that the toxic players would stay naturally in line. After all, they don't act that way at their grandmother's house, do they? Circumstances guide behavior (see the entire rest of this book) and we should be designing systems to guide their behavior into an acceptable mold.

Look at it this way: If the lack of a good hint system was causing a significant fraction of our players to quit, we'd put in a hint system. If the lack of a good curb on toxicity is causing us to have to ban some of our players, don't we have the same obligation to put in that sort of system? Even if we put it in purely financial terms, every banned player is a loss to the bottom line, losing all future revenue from them and any victims they drove out of the game. We don't want them to continue the behavior, certainly, but the optimal outcome for everyone is to have them stay in the game and within the bounds of good sportsmanship.

The other reason we want to focus on reform rather than punishment is that most of the toxicity comes from relatively normal players. Only a small fraction of players are inherently toxic and enter games with an intent to cause disruption. The rest of the toxicity in online gaming comes from relatively normal players lashing out. While we can and should aggressively ban the true villains, we can't ban the half of our playerbase who simply have an above average tendency to become frustrated in genuinely frustrating situations. Because so many of our players can go toxic under the right circumstances, design interventions intended to prevent toxicity have to be considered very carefully. This case study is about how we used interviews with toxic players to validate one intervention in Overwatch.

THE WORLD NEEDS HEROES

Overwatch is Blizzard's massively successful role-based shooter game. Instead of every player in a game having roughly the same abilities, as in a *Halo* match, players in *Overwatch* have a wide range of characters they could choose to play, from tanks to healers to pure offense. Different characters have very different strengths and weaknesses, and some characters are very weak without other players choosing good supporting characters. For example, Tank characters excelled at holding the front lines of a fight but were dependent on Support characters to heal them. Teams in Overwatch are made up of anonymous strangers but are also as interdependent as any baseball or football team.

The result was a recipe for toxicity. Players on a losing team were constantly convinced that their teammates were letting them down and would lash out. Some it was pseudo-helpful ("Why don't you play a different character?") and some was just hateful (telling others to kill themselves in online games is so popular that there's a handy acronym for it, "kys").

Blizzard's solution, introduced a year or so after the game was released, was to add a system by which players could endorse their teammates for good behavior after the game. During the planning phase of the feature, an important question came up: "What will toxic players think of the endorsement system?" After all, the system was intended to punish them for what they were doing, to encourage them to change. But if it backfired, it might make the situation even worse than before. We needed to find a way to get a picture of what the user response would be ahead of time.

THE COUNCIL OF EVIL

To investigate this, we settled on focus groups as the most appropriate method. The system itself wasn't playable, so that ruled out playtests. And we weren't worried about whether they could use the system, so usability would not have been any help. What we needed was essentially a sampling of potential user reactions to the new system, so we could anticipate the various ways players might respond after it went live. That made focus groups a practical answer: get a bunch of relevant players in a room, explain the system, then listen to their answers.

But this wasn't just any focus group. Instead, we convened the most toxic players in the Los Angeles area. Because we had access to the game's databases, we could identify the most highly reported local players and invite them to come to the studio for a chat.

I admit, I slightly chickened out and asked the studio's security people to station someone nearby during the session. Not too close, but near enough that they were available to escort a participant off campus if it came to that.

As it turns out, if I hadn't known ahead of time that there was something special about these people, I would have mistaken them for any group of highly engaged players. They were knowledgeable and enthusiastic about the game, and they participated whole heartedly in a vigorous discussion about their favorite characters and what features the game should add next. To use the standard measure of a president, you'd have happily had a beer with any of them.

GOOD CONVERSATIONS WITH BAD PLAYERS

When we steered the discussion to toxicity, however, they started to reveal some of why they were likely to be reported. In general, they had been reported for losing their tempers. In their own eyes, they had been reported out of spite by jealous teammates or opponents, but they also expressed a lot of frustration at teammates who had let them down. In their minds, they were the victims. It was the other person who had started the fight by making poor choices. They didn't have to play that particular character or miss their shots. They could have stayed with the team instead of running off on their own. The players admitted to lashing out, but only in response to something another player did.

Interestingly, even in discussions where the focus group members were themselves the victims of toxicity, they always started with a reason why the other person might have been mad. It was never out of the blue, but always "I'd gotten killed, so this guy said…" or "we were losing and…". There seemed to be a nearly universal trend that toxic behaviors formed around a core of frustration that was very human and understandable, even if its manifestation was unacceptable.

There are certainly exceptions, such as some of the sexist comments that the female members of the focus group had received or some of the racial slurs, but by and large we heard stories of anger rising out of the natural friction of a cooperative multiplayer game.

Now, a few of the participants in the focus group were genuine trolls. One gentleman liked to continuously trigger a voice line built into the game, "Is this easy mode?", implying that his opponents were much worse than he was. The line, "Is this easy mode?", was intended as an insult but he justified it to himself by saying that the line couldn't be toxic because it was built into the game. If Blizzard had put it there, how could it be bad to say it?

This was a different example of moral disengagement: the player distancing himself from his own choices by suggesting that Blizzard had established that this line was safe to say. Now, I think most people would argue that his actions were deliberately annoying and disruptive. But he had a thread of justification that let him do this and still tell himself that he was a good (or at least non-evil) person.

(There will be more on moral disengagement in a later section.)

UNEXPECTED ALLIES

Interestingly, when we got to the core of the study, asking what they thought of the proposed endorsement system, we got a shocking answer: They loved it.

Without exception, all our toxic players said they thought the system was a great idea and would improve the game. They said it would make people behave better. Furthermore, when we asked them how they personally would do under this system, they thought they would be just fine. They understood what kind of behavior would be rewarded and were confident they could do it.

This was because, in their minds, they weren't the problem. They were responding to perceived provocation from other players, even when that "provocation" was just playing a weaker character. They assumed that the system would stop other people from doing the things that would set them off. I think they also, at least at some level, recognized that they needed the crutch of a potential reward for holding their tongues when a teammate screwed up. But mostly they talked about the impact on everyone else.

We were able to go back to the *Overwatch* designers and tell them that they were good to go. Even the toxic players were onboard, or at least wouldn't initially perceive the system as a threat. By testing the system early, we contributed to the team's confidence that they had a workable solution.

PART OF THE ANSWER

In the end, the system worked, but was not a panacea. Players did behave better, with reports of abusive chat initially dropping about 40% during the first few weeks after the system was introduced. There was some reversion to normal after that, but there was still a permanent improvement.

If the system had any flaws, my personal opinion is that it was too stingy with the rewards. Gaining a high reputation through this system resulted in a few extra lootboxes per month. An active player would have to hold their temper in dozens of games every month to keep their endorsement score high enough to get the maximum reward. For comparison, the Arcade game mode gave out three lootboxes for winning ten games, a much higher rate of return. And the rewards in the lootboxes also weren't particularly special—just the same skins as could be earned or bought in other ways.

COUNTERPUNCHING

My takeaway from this and my other work on toxicity is that most toxicity comes from players who feel they have been wronged. They see themselves as responding to a provocation or an unnecessary loss and lash out. This isn't true of the worst offenders, the genuinely broken people who enter a game with intent to hurt and harm. But those are a relatively small percentage compared to the much larger population of average players striking back against provocations real and imagined.

When many of our players act badly, they're actually reacting, at least from their perspective. They didn't start the fight, the other player did by provoking them or letting them down. At the same time, they've been put into a situation where they feel they have nothing to lose. After all, in their minds they are already suffering. They're being forced to keep playing even after their teammates have let them down. In their heads, this is already an intolerable situation, and their reaction can hardly make it worse. (In reality, of course, it does make it much worse.)

The key to stopping toxicity is to stop this cycle of escalation. You cannot stop the things that provoke toxicity. Someone must lose every competitive game, raids sometimes need to wipe, and it is human nature to be frustrated with one's teammates and/or opponents. The goal of an anti-toxicity system is to help people let those little incidents go, to turn the other cheek.

By setting up a system of rewards for continued good behavior, we give them a reason to hold their tongues. If they're striking out because they think they have nothing to lose, we have to give them something to lose. Punishments such as temporary or permanent bans are only partially effective at this, but as the *Overwatch* example shows, proving rewards for being seen by your teammates as a positive force in the game can also be highly effective.

JUST TALK TO THEM

Qualitative research in general and focus groups and interviews are often looked at somewhat askance by working researchers. They're incredibly subjective tools, but that's because humans are subjective creatures. When it comes to tricky subjects for research such as toxicity, there's great value in just sitting down with the relevant players and talking to them. That doesn't mean we have to agree with them or think they're right but humanizing their perspective can enable us to build and implement more effective tools for helping both them and the entire playerbase.

There is something uniquely powerful about meeting a living example of the kinds of players you're trying to help. It is motivating and affecting, even to researchers who know intellectually that the stories they're hearing firsthand aren't necessarily universal. This comes back to my earlier point that while individual stories are not hard data, anecdotes nonetheless have emotional resonance that statistics can't capture. There's also a lot of nuances to the human experience of playing games that simply can't be captured by anything other than a conversation. So, talk to your players. They deserve you taking the time to look them in the eye and listen to their stories.

CHAPTER 23
BALANCING DESTINY

There's a tendency to call everything games researchers do a "playtest," but the real defining aspect of a playtest is that involves multiple participants playing at the same time in the lab. Where playtests really excel is when we need sheer numbers of participants to draw strong conclusions about the research question. In usability, we are generally doing deep dives on a very small number of participants. A playtest involves trading away some of that depth (we can't watch every participant closely the entire time) in exchange for volume. Playtests produce less data per individual but multiplied by many participants.

One example of a topic that benefits from volume testing are games with many options, such as different character classes or branching narrative paths. If we ran only eight participants in a game with three character classes, each class would only get played by a few people. That would not be enough feedback about each class for us to be able to act on it with confidence. Mass playtests where we run large groups through the game ensures that we have enough bodies moving through the game to give every aspect of the game a fair evaluation.

The other great advantage of volume is that we can start to use statistics on the results. In a usability test with only five people, each participant represents a full 20% of the data. A single participant with a headache can shift the results significantly. But once you start running a few dozen participants, the individual differences smooth out and the data becomes useful in a new way.

While smaller studies answer the question "will any of our players have a problem with this?", larger studies can help us predict the proportion of our players who will have a problem. We can even start to ask more subjective questions like "how fun was this character?" or "how difficult was this mission?" and get useful answers.

One of the places where playtesting is most often used in game development is on the single player campaign or story mode. It's almost a standardized service by now, essentially the same process on any title with a single player mode. But every game brings its own design innovations, and sometimes those innovations require drastic changes to the traditional approach. *Destiny*'s story missions were a good example of that, a time where a new game demanded that we update our methods to meet a new challenge.

Going into *Destiny*'s development after testing five successful *Halo* titles, we thought we knew exactly how to test single player content in a first-person shooter. You just brought in target players and ran them through the story missions in order, collecting data and feedback along the way. Done. *Destiny* was just going to be another shooter, right?

Except *Destiny* had a progression system that underlay everything you could do in the game. And by giving players choices in their gameplay, we were creating the possibility that players would have radically different levels of progression at the same point in the story.

For example, Player A only vaguely cares about the main story. He wanders off and explores, runs some side missions, does some PvP, then comes back to the next mission eventually. Player B is all about the story, so she goes straight from one mission to the next. Player A will have collected a lot more experience points and gear than Player B before playing the same content. If Player A said the next mission is too easy and player B said it's too hard, who's right?

Our solution was to split all story testing into two types: progression testing and difficulty testing. You could also think of these as "holistic" and "reductionist" testing since the former tested the game as a whole and the latter tested the individual parts.

LOOKING FOR SPIKES

In difficulty testing, we started players at each mission with a specific level of power and gear. That gave us a common frame of reference from which to judge how hard the mission was. By testing and balancing each mission against a known level of player power, we could benchmark each mission and make strong recommendations as to whether it needed to be made harder or easier.

During these playtests, players were asked to rate each mission on a scale from "Much too easy" to "Much too hard", with the middle of the scale being "About right." Ideally, in a perfectly balanced game, the first few missions would be a little too easy, most missions would be about right, and the game in general would trend from easy to hard over the playthrough without any drastic increases from one mission to the next.

An example of the kind of issue we found with this methodology was the final story mission of the Moon section of the game, the Chamber of Night, which players rated as being much more difficult than the previous mission. When we investigated further, we found that this was mostly due to one particular fight with a boss called "Telthor the Unborn." In that mission, the player finds themselves locked in a room fighting off multiple waves of enemies, with the boss serving as the final enemy. It was what is known as a "skill check," where there really was no other way to pass the room without being sufficiently good at *Destiny*'s combat. Because of the mission design, there's no way for the player to control the fight. They couldn't stay at a distance and snipe; they couldn't kill some of the enemies and retreat. They entered, the door locked, and they either won or lost.

This was the kind of sudden and unforgiving difficulty spike that causes players to quit games. Because there was no real alternative but "get good," this could have been a significant issue if it had gone undetected. In retrospect, the bad design pattern (locked room, long fight with multiple waves of enemies, no way to finesse the encounter) is obvious, but in a game as long and complex as *Destiny*, it's easy for a given moment to turn cancerous. In this case, we were able to identify the issue to the design team and they were able to make things a bit easier without changing the fundamental vision for the fight. Telthor was still there and still a challenge in the final version of the game, but no longer a hard block.

HIGH EXPECTATIONS

In progression testing, we started players from the beginning and allowed them to play as they wished. They earned XP at the normal rate and received new gear from enemies and rewards as they naturally would. This was more or less the experience that players would have in the shipped game. These were very long extended playtests, lasting one to two days, and allowed players to start at the beginning of the game and progress normally, as they would after release.

After each playtest, we'd compare the average level players had reached when they started each mission to the level the designers predicted they would. In our early testing, players kept up with the intended level for the first few missions but then began to fall behind. Ideally, the amount of experience players received in each mission should have naturally left them at the right level for the next mission, but that wasn't happening the way we thought it would. Part of this was due to insufficient rewards, but we also failed to anticipate how single-minded players would be about pushing through the story. Our participants were experienced shooter players and they quite reasonably tried to play our story missions as if it were a *Halo* campaign: a single linear game mode rather than one activity among many. They didn't stop to smell (and loot) the roses, so they became more and more underleveled as they progressed.

This phenomenon really caused problems when we had a large step up in expected level between the final Venus mission and the first Mars mission. The story designers thought players would notice the higher required levels in the UI and go do non-story activities for a while to gain more levels before returning to finish the campaign. Our shooter players, on the other hand, thought they were supposed to just move through the entire story sequentially and never noticed the higher level requirements. They just thought the game had gotten really hard all of a sudden.

The attitude of our traditional shooter players towards difficulty caused other problems *Destiny*'s playtesting. In RPGs, it's common for players to occasionally encounter enemies that are too high level for them, and experienced RPG gamers know that they're not supposed to be going toe to toe with those enemies. They understand that they're supposed to sneak past, or maybe go away and come back later when they're higher level themselves. But FPS players were accustomed to every enemy being their level. If you encountered an enemy in a *Halo* mission, for example, it was something you were supposed to be able to kill. It might be hard, but it was a purposefully built and tuned fight that you could learn to beat. "Go away and come back later when you're stronger" was just not a thing in most FPS games. This resulted in a lot of our participants fighting enemies much too hard for them. The enemy was in front of them, so they must be supposed to fight it.

One of the early designs for *Destiny* involved having areas with differing enemy levels adjacent to each other, with a few strong enemies called "bouncers" at the transition point. The idea was that players would come close to the boundary, encounter the bouncers, then turn away and stick to the easier enemies who were appropriately matched to them. Unfortunately, that wasn't what our playtesters did at all. Instead, they dug in and kept fighting the bouncers, dying dozens of times. The enemy was there, it was hard, but they figured it must be a bossfight or something. The idea of turning away and leaving that enemy alone was completely alien to the traditional shooter mindset. A skull icon over an enemy's head just meant a chance for glory, not the warning sticker that it would be for an MMO or RPG player.

We ended up doing some work to better message the change in required level, encouraging players more explicitly to try other things before finishing the story. We also made it so that once you landed on a planet, the enemies were pretty much all the same level.

(A similar phenomenon was discovered during the development of the *Shadowrun* game for the Xbox 360, which used both guns and magic abilities. When the designers created scenarios designed to encourage players to use their magic, the players just decided that it was just a very hard shooter game. The only way we could force players out of a shooter mindset was to make it literally impossible to progress without using abilities, which in turn created a lot of unnecessary frustration.)

In some ways, this player mindset made *Destiny* a better game. We were forced to make the game a shooter first and an RPG second. This was always the official plan, and the game was deliberately marketed as a "shared world shooter" rather than an MMORPG. But there was a constant temptation to tune things more to the MMO end of the spectrum than the shooter side. Playtesting (and player stubbornness) highlighted those moments where we fell into relying on the player to win fights with stats rather than skill.

TWO PERSPECTIVES, ONE GAME

The combination of these two kinds of testing was an essential component of how *Destiny*'s story was polished. Both methods shared the same fundamentals (put players in front of the campaign, see what happens) with slightly different circumstances. Progression testing ensured that players were the right level when they reached a mission, and difficulty testing ensured that they were appropriately challenged once they got there.

Had we only done one method, the game would have been broken. If we'd done just difficulty testing, the missions would have been well-designed but players would have been crushed or bored, depending on their level. If we'd done just progression testing, we wouldn't have been able to tune the individual missions because each player would have reached that mission at a different power level, and we wouldn't have had enough data to draw firm conclusions.

NEW IDEAS

Real innovation in user research should be driven by the game. The research plan for *Destiny* started as an iteration of how we tested *Halo*, but it rapidly evolved once *Destiny's* unique gameplay came into focus. The game simply couldn't be tested the way our prior games had, and we therefore had to invent new approaches to match the new gameplay.

People always ask me "where do you think games research will be in five years?" and assume that the answer will have something to do with new technologies or testing paradigms. But the answer is much simpler: We'll go where our games go. There's no need to push for innovation unilaterally; just trying to keep up with our partners provides more than enough direction. As long as the games industry innovates, researchers inevitably will too.

CHAPTER 24
CHEATING THE TRIALS OF OSIRIS

SCALE VS CONTROL

Surveys are one of the only tools available to games researchers that scales really well because the researcher doesn't have to be present when the data is being collected. When done correctly, surveys gain us almost all the benefits of interviews or focus groups, with the added plus of being fully automated. Surveying a thousand people can take less time than interviewing a half dozen.

The price of all that beautiful free data is that the researcher doesn't have direct control of how the player fills the survey out. For all we know, the person answering the survey might not be the one who played the game. There's no way of knowing who's on the other side of the screen and how seriously they're taking a survey. These days, they might not even be a person at all; there are lots of bots to fill out surveys in hopes of winning prizes. The trade-off for scaling is a lack of hands-on control.

Therefore, the core design constraint of surveys becomes not "how do I ask the questions I want to know about?" but instead, "how do I ask the questions in a way that best extracts true responses from the noise?" We want to write a survey so clear, so foolproof that the lack of control isn't an issue. A good survey runs on rails, a machine to separate signal from noise.

One of my favorite research tools is targeting surveys based on gameplay data. By taking the detailed data we log for every player and choosing who to contact, we can learn about important subpopulations in our games that would normally be too rare to investigate blindly. And we then compare their answers back against their demonstrated behavior to understand where they're telling the truth and where they're bending it a little.

The example below includes both of these attributes. It's a situation where we used behavioral data to target a specific subset of our players, then built a survey carefully structured to draw out honest answers from a population not known for their honesty.

In 2015, Bungie introduced a new feature into *Destiny*, the Trials of Osiris. This was a new Player vs. Player (PvP) mode intended to provide a high skill competitive experience and really good loot.

It was simultaneously a great success and opened the door to players cheating on a scale that we'd never seen before in the game. It also created a unique research opportunity.

Here's what happened.

THE NEW GAME MODE

The core mechanic for Trials was that players bought a ticket to participate, and they then played competitive matches until they either won nine games or lost three games. If they lost three games, they were done and had to buy another ticket to try again. But if they won nine games with two losses or less, they got to fly to a cool new destination on Mercury and open a giant golden chest, receiving valuable top-end weapons and armor.

The new mode was an immediate hit, creating a way for competitive players to get high quality loot and bragging rights. However, the mode also unleashed a giant wave of cheating. Because players only had to win a few games to get amazing loot, they only had to put their finger on the scale once or twice to receive great rewards.

The primary method of cheating was a form of "queue dodging." *Destiny* at the time had fairly long loading screens as players joined a multiplayer game, ensuring smooth gameplay during the match by making sure everything was loaded into memory beforehand. As they waited on the loading screen, players used the mission roster to inspect their opponents to see what kind of equipment they were using. They weren't able to see the other players' skill rankings directly, but by looking at their gear they could get a sense of how accomplished the other players were. If the player had better gear than they did, the cheating team would leave the match before it technically began. Because they hadn't actually joined the game yet, this was not counted as a loss for them. The other team would arrive in an empty arena and be granted a win, and the cheaters could queue up for a new match against a hopefully less challenging set of opponents.

It was a subtle edge, but one that allowed thousands of players to win the Trials without actually competing fairly against the field. They were artificially constraining the teams they would play against, making the mode much easier than the designers had intended.

The problems were immediately obvious after the first weekend of Trials matches. The development team at Bungie reacted quickly, banning all the players who participated in the misbehavior and communicating to the playerbase that this behavior would not be tolerated.

THE OPPORTUNITY

The immediate issue had been addressed, but a unique window for user research had been created. Most games don't have a ton of cheaters. They do periodic "ban waves" of a few dozen or even few hundred players, but the small numbers and spacing over time make them a tricky population to study. On top of that, most accounts banned tend to be either new players or bots, so they're not particularly interesting to talk to (or, for that matter, interested in talking to the dev team).

But in this case, we'd penalized literally thousands of long-time human players for cheating at the same time. This was a golden opportunity to study a large population of proven cheaters right after the incident. Because there were also hundreds of thousands of legitimate Trials players, we had an easy "control" population to compare the cheaters against as well. It was a perfect laboratory for studying the differences between those who chose to cheat and those who didn't.

The most interesting thing was that when we looked at their gameplay data, there wasn't much difference. The cheaters and non-cheaters had previously played similar game modes for similar amounts of time and had similar levels of skill. One of our hypotheses had been that the cheaters were lower skilled players trying to steal rewards they weren't good enough to earn. It was a comforting idea, but the evidence didn't line up. The difference between cheaters and honest players wasn't visible in their pre-cheating behavior.

We needed more information, the kind we could only get by actually talking to our cheaters.

THE SURVEY

Because the cheaters were scattered all over the globe, we had to use a survey to investigate rather than bring them into the studio. That would let us reach a large audience, but the fact that they'd be filling it out at home meant that it wouldn't be a captive audience. (Not that they're ever really captive, but you know what I mean.)

The biggest challenge was that the sensitivity of the subject matter meant respondents were likely to quit the survey if we accused them directly of misbehavior. Therefore, we had to structure the survey in an order specifically designed to ease them into the topic and extract as much information from them as possible before they might quit in a huff.

We started with very general questions about the game, overall opinions, what they liked and disliked about *Destiny* as a whole. This was mostly to get them warmed up, into the rhythm of answering questions, but it would also give us a chance to see if any of their overall attitudes about the game differed. As it turned out, attitudes towards the game as a whole were very similar in both the banned players and the control group. This lined up with their pre-Trials gameplay data, since we'd assume that players with radically different attitudes towards the game would have radically different play habits and vice versa.

Eventually, we started to carefully walk the respondents through a set of progressively more pointed questions, paying special attention to the order so that we didn't risk spooking them early. To avoid contamination, during this survey we disabled the ability to go backwards to edit or remove their earlier answers.

First, we asked how common they thought cheating was in *Destiny*.

Then we asked if they had ever seen anyone cheat.

Then we asked if any of their friends had cheated.

Then we asked if they personally had cheated.

Then we asked if they'd ever been banned for cheating.

Finally, we dropped the bomb and informed them that we knew that their account had been banned. We carefully did not say they were cheaters, but just stated the bare fact of the ban. Note the phrasing of "the account had been banned." We didn't directly accuse them as a human being of doing anything wrong. We wanted to leave the door open (at least in their own heads) to having been unjustly accused.

Then we asked the million-dollar question:

Why did you do the thing that led to your account being banned?

This was the big question, the point of the study, but there was one more major section that you need to understand first before we can talk about the results.

MORAL DISENGAGEMENT

Before we started asking directly about cheating, we had players fill out a "moral disengagement scale." This is a set of questions social psychologists use to understand whether someone tends to distance themselves from their own decisions. Each question on the scale is meant to measure the respondent's likelihood to use certain mental strategies to avoid taking personal responsibility. For example, one way to separate yourself from your actions is to claim that the decision was actually made by someone else, or that the person who was impacted wasn't really hurt.

The questions took the form of a set of statements such as "it's alright to lie to keep your friends out of trouble" and players were asked to rate each statement on a scale from "Strongly disagree" to "Strongly agree."

I was floored by the results, especially how different the banned and non-banned players' answers were:

> 36% of the banned players agreed with the statement "People who get mistreated have usually done something to bring it on themselves", compared to only 16% of the non-banned Trial players.
>
> 20% of the banned players agreed that "People cannot be blamed for doing things that are technically wrong when all their friends are doing it too", with only 8% of the non-banned players agreeing.

Most strikingly, given the social nature of this particular exploit, 29% of the banned players agreed that "People cannot be blamed for misbehaving if their friends pressured them into it," compared to 8% of the control players.

I honestly didn't expect much from this part of the survey. Really, the questions seemed so obvious, addressing the kind of moral failures and excuses that even schoolchildren know are wrong. And some of the banned players did respond with the correct answers. But in aggregate, the answers showed that there was an overall difference in how our banned and unbanned players thought about cheating.

PLEADING NOT GUILTY

As it turned out, one of the reasons so many people cheated in Trials was that the particular cheat they were using was really easy to justify. By queuing up for a game, then quickly inspecting the enemy team's equipment before the match fully loaded them onto the map and preemptively quitting if the other team had better equipment, they would avoid the game without taking a loss, and hand the opposing team a win. It was a selfish choice, but not one that struck them as directly hurtful to the other players.

Part of what made this strategy so interesting from a moral perspective is that the entire team had to do it more or less simultaneously. Once one player on a team quit, the others were faced with the choice of either quitting as well or staying in the match. If they stayed, they'd be at a numerical disadvantage and almost guaranteed a loss. This introduced a strong element of peer pressure and helped a lot of players go along with something they might not have done if they were playing alone.

When we analyzed players' stated reasons for their actions, we saw every one of the known moral disengagement strategies in use by at least some of the players.

Here are some categories of reasons what players told us for why they cheated and how they line up with the moral disengagement strategies:[1]

> *"I was just doing it to help my friend get better gear."* The players who said this were claiming a moral justification for what they did.
>
> *"It wasn't cheating, it was just 'queue dodging'"* - This was an example of euphemistic labeling. By calling their actions something other than cheating, they made them more acceptable.
>
> *"If we weren't supposed to do it, it shouldn't have been possible to do it from the game UI."* - This was attribution of blame. The players who tried this route were reducing their own culpability by saying it was the developers' responsibility to prevent the action.
>
> *"The other team won the game, so no one was really hurt."* - Players who tried this were minimizing consequences. Their actions did have a negative consequence because they were skipping over potential losses so they could get to players they could beat. They were improving their own odds but lowering the odds of other players.
>
> *"Once my friend quit, I had to either quit or lose the game."* - The group nature of this particular kind of queue dodging led to a lot of players using a displacement of responsibility strategy. While it might have been true if they'd only done it once, the people who were banned in this case had done many times.

Being put in a bad situation by your friends once is understandable but going back for more is clearly a choice.

"It's not like we were ddos-ing or hacking." - Some of our players engaged in advantageous comparison strategy, saying that their actions hadn't been that bad compared to other possibilities.

"We saw another team doing it first, so we just tried it to see what would happen." - Similar to the "I was just following my friends" strategy, the diffusion of responsibility approach tried to spread the blame around. The thing is, we didn't ban anyone who tried it once; we banned people who had an ongoing pattern of queue dodging.

Though players had a lot of different stated reasons for cheating, they all came down to the same thing. They were ways for the player to still think of themselves as a good person who had just happened to do a bad thing for reasons. They separated the good person from the bad action, letting them keep both their self-image and their ill-gotten loot.

Interestingly, after all that thoughtful structure intended to protect the survey from people dropping out early, we actually had far fewer respondents quit than we anticipated. All our precautions to ease them into the scary questions about their own actions were probably unnecessary, precisely because of their moral disengagement. After all, they saw themselves as good people who had sufficient reasons for technically breaking the rules and were more than happy to explain to us why they were completely justified.

TAKEAWAYS

First, cheaters were hard to separate from the normal population. As I've said before, we tend to think of our bad actors as supervillains who are obviously different from normal people. However, outside of behaviors and attitudes specifically related to their ban, these were perfectly normal players. In fact, they were in many ways above average players. They were passionate about the game, spent their time and money on it, and were active in the community. They posted on the forums, founded clans, and played with their friends like anyone else. Their behavior in this case was certainly unacceptable and they did deserve their bans, but if we could theoretically help them stay honest, they were potentially valuable members of the community.

Second, almost no one said "yes, I'm a cheating cheater who cheated because I wanted the rewards." Instead, they found ways to justify it to themselves, to maintain a positive self-image while also doing something they know they're not supposed to. In their heads, they've found a way to square the circle, to create a moral exception that applies to their particular circumstance. This has the interesting implication that if we make it harder for players to justify their cheating, they'll be less likely to cheat. In this case, players were using an in-game menu option to leave the games. If that menu item were disabled, the only way to disconnect from the game would be to unplug their Xbox from the internet. Because that's a much more overt action, it's a lot harder to justify and fewer people would do it. While we can't entirely remove the base motivation to cheat, we can raise the amount of mental work players have to do to talk themselves into it.

Finally, surveys deserve more respect than they get. A lot of people assume that because surveys are self-administered, players will lie. It's true that players will slightly skew their responses, but players will also confess to remarkable things. A sizable minority of the survey's respondents did come out and said "yes, I've been banned for cheating" when asked. And we saw in their answers on the moral disengagement scale that they tended to reveal a lot more about themselves than they knew.

Surveys aren't a perfect tool, but their reach and scale guarantee them a permanent place in a researcher's kit.

CHAPTER 25
EXTRACTING TRUTH FROM THE INTERNET

One common refrain in the industry is "we don't need researchers, we talk to our players on the internet all the time." However, the players who participate in internet discussions are not anything like a representative sample of all players. The general rule of thumb is that approximately 10% of all players for a game will even visit the forums, and only 1% will make a post or comment of their own. When a developer listens to their forums, they're listening to their most hardcore and involved players. To put some numbers around this: When I looked at *Halo* players, I found that those who participated on the forums played approximately three times as many hours as the average player. Just as we can't rely solely on internal studio opinions, relying on forums will lead us to design a game around a very small and specialized audience.

Even so, online forums (and Twitter, Reddit, YouTube, etc.) have a role to play in user research: *inspiration*. The correct response to a problem reported online (be it forum post, tweet, viral video, etc.) is to wonder how common it is. Every comment is true; it's just that some are true for more people than others. If someone says a change in the game ruined their experience, then we have to take that as a truth for them. But the next step for a researcher is to investigate, to see what the larger patterns are, and whether this particular complaint rises to the level of action.

THE MYTH OF THE MYTHOCLAST

When the Mythoclast rifle was first introduced in *Destiny 1*, there was a great outcry online saying that the weapon was too powerful in PvP and was ruining all competitive multiplayer matches. Rather than do an emergency patch, we investigated to see how common the problem actually was. We discovered that only a few hundred players had the gun at the time out of a population of literally millions of active players, and that it was only involved in a fraction of a percent of competitive matches. The gun was still unbalanced, but the problem was small enough that we could take an extra week or two to make a thoughtful balance change rather than a rushed fix that risked making things worse.

RED VS. BLUE

However, even though a lot of online complaints are overblown or unrepresentative, every once in a while they turn out to be completely true. My favorite example of this was when I was working on *Halo 2*. One of the Bungie developers came to me after the game had been out for a while and told me that there was a guy on the forums who thought the red team was winning more than the blue team. He asked me to check and find out if they're right. On the face of it, this was ridiculous. Color in *Halo 2* was purely cosmetic, and even on the asymmetric maps the colors were assigned randomly. (e.g., Red didn't always start on the left, Blue wasn't always on defense, and so on.) So, any difference in win rates should have been nothing but noise. But this player had recorded the outcome of hundreds of his own games and found a small but consistent difference. Rather than take his comment as proof in itself, we used it as the jumping-off point for our own investigation. When we conducted a statistical analysis, we did indeed find that for a few weeks there had been a small (~2%) benefit to being on the Red team. Within the game, it was still true that both colors swapped starting places and time on offense and defense equally, Red was slightly more likely to win.

After sharing this finding around the studio, one of the engineers came forward to admit that he'd slightly tweaked how colors were assigned in multiplayer. While the matchmaking algorithm tried to create two equally balanced teams, it was inevitable that someone in the match would have the highest individual skill rating. This engineer had assumed that being Red was actually a slight *disadvantage*, because the brighter color would make the Red players easier to spot and shoot. Therefore, the team with the highest skilled player would always be assigned to Red to even things out. It was the team, not the color, that had the advantage. We went back to truly random color assignment and the issue was resolved.

One important thing about this story is that the player gathered actual evidence. He didn't have as much data as the studio, of course, but he came to the table with something more than just a feeling. The better-documented the phenomenon, the more likely it is to be taken seriously.

THE WI FLAG

Another great example of accurate forum feedback is the so-called "Wi Flag" in *Asheron's Call*. For years, some players in *Asheron's Call* had complained that the game was out to get them. They said that enemies would target them more than anyone else. Engineers at Turbine, the game's developer, investigated and said that they had checked the random number generator and were confident that the game wasn't playing with loaded dice. And yet, players and even some Turbine employees reported that they were being picked on. Whenever there was an ambiguous situation and an enemy could "choose" among several potential targets, some players said that enemies always singled them out, running past closer players to hunt them in particular. They were apparently cursed.

Eventually, after this had gone on for several years and multiple investigations had turned up nothing, one of the engineers discovered that while the game did more or less randomly choose who should be targeted from a list, the *order* of the players on the list was determined by the player's unique ID number in the database. Under certain circumstances, the player at the top of the list had a much higher chance to be targeted than anyone else. The players had indeed picked up on a flaw in the randomness, and they really were being persecuted by the algorithm.

Note that in all of these cases, the community complaints didn't lead directly to changes in the game. Instead, in every case, community concerns inspired a systematic investigation and the investigation led to the correct decision. The people who play on the forums are too different from the average player, and what's good for them is not always good for the game.

Forum dwellers and other online commenters are massively unrepresentative of the playerbase as a whole, but that doesn't necessarily make them wrong. A smart researcher can use the internet noise the same way they use their personal experiences and the anecdotes of their friends and coworkers: as inspiration for more objective research projects that can find the real truth.

CHAPTER 26
FABLE'S GOLDEN PATH

Even after the tutorial is over, games need to keep teaching and leading their players. Hint systems, waypoints, and even more direct tools are necessary to guide players through the game, but both players and designers often resent the necessity of this kind of hand-holding. The *Fable* and *Destiny* examples below are examples of how we wrestled with both the need and the resentment for guidance in the playtest lab.

Fable was arguably the premier fantasy RPG of the original Xbox. It offered an amazing variety of character choices and was one of the first games to give players the ability to become either evil or good and have that choice reflected in your character's appearance.

One aspect of the game was hotly debated during development. There was a glowing golden line visible on the ground in front of you, leading towards your next objective. Players weren't required to follow the line to play, but it was always there, telling you in which direction the main story lay. Sure, you could wander off and explore, but the glowing line implied that only one direction was correct.

In early playtesting, players complained bitterly that the line was too demanding. It seemed to remove all choice from the game, constantly driving the player towards the next step in the main quest and discouraging exploration. In a game that strove to be about individualism, the golden line was seen as a mandate for conformity. Some of the developers even felt the same way, that the line was working against the vision of the game.

The solution, it turned out, was not to remove the line. Instead, they added a setting in the menu that let the player choose to dim or remove the line, and a pop-up message told the player about the setting early on. Suddenly, there were no more complaints about the line being too bright or too leading but most importantly, *no one in our playtests turned the line off*. Just having the ability to remove the line was enough. Everyone left it on by choice.

It's not the instructional content most people object to when learning a new game, it's the lack of choice. A good tutorial or hint system is one that guides the player as completely as they need, while offering them the opportunity to turn away from the path. (Even if a player did turn off the line in this example, they could always just turn it back on if they got lost.)

This was also a great example of how not all features have to be used to be useful. Even if very few players ever turned off the line, the ability to do so provided value to a larger segment of the playerbase. We are not a logical species, so a good design will not always be logical either.

Finally, you'll note that the ultimate solution wasn't the one that the players actually asked for. The line was legitimately bothering them, but removing it wasn't the right design decision. Their feedback did help identify a problem, but the actual solution came from the experience and creativity of the design team.

A similar debate occurred during the development of *Destiny 1*. Like many open world or RPG games, *Destiny* had visible waypoints in the UI that showed players the next target location. Players, naturally enough, tended to go straight towards the next beacon without deviating much. The studio had built a beautiful, expansive game world and players were walking across it in boring straight lines.

This led to a lot of heated discussion on the design team. As one of the senior engineers put it, "we didn't build the most powerful server cluster in gaming so players could walk from waypoint to waypoint."

And yet when we hid the waypoints, the game became much less fun. There was a fine line between "free to explore" and "hopelessly lost." Because every map in *Destiny* was built to be reused in different missions, they didn't naturally funnel the player in the right direction the way *Halo*'s maps had. *Halo* didn't need as many waypoints because the missions were relatively linear, and players could only get so lost. We also had little tricks built into *Halo*'s map designs, like having the player jump down a small cliff when moving in the correct direction. Once they were down, they couldn't jump back up and were therefore forced onwards in the mission. *Destiny* was a different kind of game with a different kind of map, and therefore required more prominent waypoints to be navigable.

The *Fable* team chose to keep the golden line, and *Destiny* kept its waypoints. Being lost is an interesting idea artistically, but I can count on one hand the number of times a game has successfully made being lost a fun experience. Momentary confusion is fine, puzzles are fine, but in my experience most players have very little tolerance for extended periods of feeling stupid.

The good news is that players will tell you when it's not working. When they do, the duty of the research and the designers is to believe the feedback and being willing to sacrifice a little of their artistic vision for the sake of a good player experience.

EPILOGUE - GETTING A JOB IN GAMES RESEARCH

Working in the games industry is a dream job for a lot of people, but the path into the industry isn't always as clear for researchers as it is for more traditional roles such as coders or animators. However, as someone who's hired a lot of researchers over the years, there are some general pieces of advice that I believe apply to anyone looking to get their first job in this field. By strange coincidence, these also mirror my own journey into the industry.

1. LEARN THE TECHNICAL SKILLS

Most of the fundamental skills required to be successful as an entry-level games user researcher are universal research skills, not specific to games. This is awesome, because it means that we can hire researchers from a wider variety of backgrounds and expect that their prior experience and skills will still apply. Also, it means that there are more resources for a candidate to learn from. The number of books specifically written about usability testing for games is fairly limited, but usability testing in general has had hundreds of books written about it. Someone interested in games research can learn most of the necessary technical skills without ever setting foot in a game studio.

Some of the core disciplines I'd expect any researcher to have experience in are:

- Statistics
- Experimental design
- Survey design
- Usability test design and moderation
- Research ethics
- Data visualization

To be clear, I'm not saying a candidate has to be a master researcher before they can get an entry level job. But everything that has to be taught after hiring takes time and bandwidth that would be better spent on actually improving our games. Making the effort to build your arsenal before applying shows the attitude that hiring managers look for.

2. DO THE WORK

There is nothing stopping anyone reading this from going out and doing games research right now. (I'd selfishly suggest finishing the book first, but it's up to you.) As I hope I've made clear in the rest of this book, the core elements of games user research are not complicated: Player, game, and observer. While you may not be employed on the game you're testing, you can go through the motions as if you were and begin learning the craft on your own. Really, just watch someone play and take good notes and you'll be on the right path.

As to what game to do research on, there are a million early access games on Steam or Itch.io that are both done enough to be playable and early enough to have plenty of rough areas. Pick any one that at least potentially could be played for an hour without instruction or crippling bugs.

Your studies don't have to be miracles of scientific rigor. Put the game on a laptop, take it to the local coffee shop, and offer to pay for a drink for anyone who will spend 20 minutes playing. Or make a survey in a free online survey tool and post it on an online game forum. These don't have to be rocket science, and there's immense value in going through the process firsthand.

As a plus, the work you do this way can be a significant part of your portfolio when you come to apply for an actual industry job. One of the nicer things about the games industry is that it doesn't really distinguish between professional and amateur work. Plenty of breakout hits in gaming in the past few years have come from independent developers and their hobby projects. Similarly, there have been plenty of solid research projects by graduate students or hobbyists that have been well received by the games research community.

Part of what got me my first job in the industry was having been an administrator on an amateur MUD (Multi-User Dungeon, an old type of text-based MMO). I'd been responsible for designing the new player area, and I had a habit of invisibly watching new players move through the initial experience of my MUD. I'd see where they got stuck, where they got lost, where they quit, and then I'd make modifications to improve things. It wasn't science or professional game development, but it was a genuine, demonstrated interest in understanding players and improving their experience.

3. PUT YOUR WORK OUT THERE

Personally, I'm horrible at networking and I do much better when I let my work make introductions for me. My personal entry into the industry came from publishing an article, "Behavioral Game Design," on a games industry website while I was in graduate school. It garnered a fair bit of attention and led to Microsoft's research team contacting me for a potential job. Before they reached out, I had no idea that games user research was a career option. My work had gone into a place that I didn't know existed and touched people I'd never have thought to contact.

A similar thing happened with my later job at Blizzard. I gave a talk on my *Halo* work at a conference in 2010, just sharing what I'd done and learned without any particular goal. Six years later, someone who'd been sitting in that audience that day was in a position to start up a new research team and thought of me.

My work has always been my best ambassador, and I think the same is true for most people. Even a highly industrious person can only mail out so many resumes, but a well written article or a video can easily go viral within a small, tightly networked professional community like games research.

Don't worry if the sample work isn't perfect. Someone coming from outside the industry will always miss some of the nuances. The key is to demonstrate two things: a passion for games and the ability to translate your research skills to this domain. Most researchers in the industry were trained in more traditional fields and then migrated into games. Their successful transition into this industry is determined by their flexibility—their ability to take what was learned in real sciences like psychology or sociology or even geology and apply it to this weird new world.

Not incidentally, doing something on your own and putting your work out there shows good hustle. It demonstrates effort and passion, which are essential to thriving in games.

4. WORK FOR A BIG PUBLISHER

This is probably my most controversial recommendation for new folks entering the industry. There's a bit of punk glamour to being an indie developer, and a lot of people come into the industry wanting to make their own ideas happen instead of being one of a thousand people working on an established AAA title.

However, the large publishers have a lot to recommend them, especially for new researchers. Big publishers generally have large research teams with well-polished training programs that serve as an effective finishing school for new researchers. At a smaller company with one or two researchers, training tends to be either non-existent or monkey-see-monkey-do. That can work, but it's a much more difficult road.

Large publishers also tend to work on a variety of games at the same time, and a researcher there can build up experience testing a lot of different genres in just a few years. A smaller studio might only make a single title or a single type of title, providing a much narrower window into the industry.

EXPERTISE, PASSION, AND BEING A REAL GAMER

Note that being an expert gamer is not on this list. One of the biggest mistakes people make when considering becoming a games researcher is thinking that they have to be a master gamer to qualify. That's not true for games in general and especially not true about expertise in the particular games the studio makes. I'm personally terrible at the shooter games that have made up the majority of my career. I play them and enjoy them, but I'm not particularly good at them. Playing games is a different skill set than making games, so don't hold yourself back from applying for a job because you haven't hit platinum rank or some other arbitrary skill floor. Remember, half of all players are by definition below average, and they deserve someone in the studio to speak for them, too.

A passion for games is required, though. You have to have a fire for the medium to survive and thrive in the industry. You have to play something for fun, even if it's the fluffiest hypercasual mobile game. Don't be ashamed of your taste in games, either. When you interview in a studio that makes the toughest competitive fighting game, look them straight in the eye and tell them about all the hours you spent playing *Animal Crossing*. The most likely reaction you'll hear is "Oh, I love that game!" What you play is less important than being part of the larger gaming tribe.

Similarly, it's also important to speak the language. Gamers are an entire subculture, and those of us who work in the industry live and breathe that culture. To be effective, a researcher has to get the jokes, use the right code words, and show that they're part of the in-group. Playing a wide variety of games enough to understand the basics and the terminology is important. Your coworkers will talk about their work in a shorthand that is pretty impenetrable to anyone who isn't a gamer. They'll say they're building a "Patchwerk-type boss fight" or a "trench run" and you won't want to mark yourself as an outsider by having to ask for an explanation. You don't even have to play all the games yourself. Game streaming services and YouTube are wonderful resources for learning about new games and keeping up with the lingo.

One point that shouldn't need to be said: You should at least try the game the studio makes before you speak to anyone from the studio. You don't have to love it, finish it, or even be good at it, but you have to play it. It's amazing how many applicants don't bother to play the game they're applying to work on. This is the thing you'll be putting in hours every week on, you have to at least make sure you don't hate it and that it will reflect well upon you to have it on your resume. It also shows you care about the job and aren't just firing off resumes at random. This is particularly true of any studio that offers a play-for-free version of their game. If I interview someone about a position on my team and they haven't tried the game, the interview's over. Our mouths will keep moving, but there's no chance I would hire someone who won't put in that minimal effort.

WHY YOU SHOULDN'T WORK IN GAMES

I love working in games. It's what I've done my entire professional career and I have trouble imagining myself doing anything else. However, there are some major drawbacks to a career in games that a prospective researcher should keep in mind.

First, there are a lot of structural downsides to working in games. The games industry is unstable compared to more mature businesses. Appropriately enough, it's somewhere in between the relative solidity of traditional software development and the chaos of a pure entertainment field like pop music or making movies. Many studios are only a single failed game away from bankruptcy, and few people make it through their careers without experiencing at least one layoff. This is not a good industry for people who want to retire from the same company they started with.

On a similar note, games jobs tend to pay less than equivalent positions in productivity software firms. To put it bluntly, there's a lot more people who want to work in games than there are jobs, and that creates a permanent downward pressure on wages. There are exceptions, but by and large games jobs pay about 20% less. As a young person straight out of school, that might not seem like a big deal, but it's tough on families. If objective financial success matters to you, this is probably not your industry. Some studios and developers do very well, but they're the exception rather than the rule.

It's also important to remember that the industry is relatively small. There are fewer game companies than other software companies and we're mostly centered in a few major cities like Seattle, Austin, Vancouver, B.C., Los Angeles, and Montreal. Therefore, you will have fewer choices of where to work and live. Again, for a young single person this might seem doable, but it could make balancing careers with a spouse more difficult. Due to the tight secrecy of game development, not all studios are OK with working remotely. If you need flexibility in where and how you work, working in games may not be ideal.

Finally, loving games is necessary, but not sufficient. For all the reasons mentioned above, games are not an industry anyone should work in by accident. If someone just wants to make a living, there are much easier and more stable ways to do so. To thrive in the industry, working on games has to be special enough be worth all the other issues.

This passion for games also carries with it the potential for exploitation. There's a slippery slope from "I'm willing to be paid a little less to work in an industry I love" to outright exploitation. This is not a very unionized industry, so it's unfortunately up to individual employees to draw the line beyond which they won't go. I advise working that line out ahead of time, because it can be tough to say "no" in the moment if you haven't already made up your mind.

Because of all those issues (and plenty of others), careers in games also tend to be short. The average tenure in the industry is about five years. It's relatively rare for a studio to last more than a decade. There's nothing wrong with trying a career path and deciding it's not for you, but I didn't bet everything on games and neither should you. I got a real degree that could be used for both games and other things and lived in places where there were other employment options besides games. Working in games is great, but it's unlikely to be your forever home. Don't burn your bridges back to the real world.

If you want to just make games, you're probably better off as a hobbyist. Get a real job, make games for fun on your own time, and be happy. You can do that anywhere, choose your own collaborators, and make things you're proud of. That is every bit as valid as what I've done. If making games is what matters to you, it's perfectly possible to do that without making the industry your career.

WHY I WORK IN GAMES

When I walk into my studio, I know that every coworker is a true believer. We all chose this industry because we love the medium and have worked hard to be here. There are no disinterested clock punchers, just incredibly smart, passionate, and creative people. When I do my job correctly, I help them to be even better, to ship a game that's slightly more fun than it would have been without me.

For me, games user research is a chance to apply my skills in a medium I love and to touch a lot of lives in a small way. My games themselves are ephemeral bits of popular culture, but the players and their experiences are real. I have heard so many stories from players about how they bonded with their parents over a game, met their spouse online, and discovered their own real strengths meeting virtual challenges. My games have been played by hundreds of millions of people, and I'm proud of having made each of them a little bit happier.

NOTES

9. WHY I HATE FUN

1. This chapter originally appeared as an article at GamesIndustry.biz and has been reprinted with permission.

21. THE TIME I TRIED TO RUIN HALO 2

1. This chapter originally appeared as a feature at Polygon.com and has been reprinted with permission.

24. CHEATING THE TRIALS OF OSIRIS

1. These specific quotes are examples created by me to illustrate each strategy, but are representative of what we found in the survey.

ABOUT THE AUTHOR

John Hopson has been a researcher in the games industry for twenty years, working on some of the biggest franchises in gaming, including *Halo, Destiny, Age of Empires, Overwatch, World of Warcraft, Hearthstone, StarCraft, Diablo, Guild Wars,* and *Lineage.* He holds a doctorate in experimental psychology from Duke University.

https://secretscienceofgames.com/